# FISHING SECRETS

*The life and times of A present day
Charter Fishing Captain.*

## CAPTAIN DALE A. LAURIN SR.

authorHOUSE®

*AuthorHouse™*
*1663 Liberty Drive*
*Bloomington, IN 47403*
*www.authorhouse.com*
*Phone: 1-800-839-8640*

*Published by AuthorHouse 12/09/2013*

*ISBN: 978-1-4918-4117-4 (sc)*
*ISBN: 978-1-4918-4116-7 (e)*

*Library of Congress Control Number: 2013922148*

*Any people depicted in stock imagery provided by Thinkstock are models,*
*and such images are being used for illustrative purposes only.*
*Certain stock imagery* © *Thinkstock.*

*This book is printed on acid-free paper.*

# Contents

# AUTHOR'S NOTE

People constantly ask me: Are there really secrets to fishing? My answer is yes! But not the type of secrets you may think.

It was in the stars that I became a guide and charter fishing captain. It has allowed me to truly help others become fishermen and teach others how to cope with life. Like Domino's, the passion continues for a "Line In The Water".

# PREFACE

Let me begin before I begin.

This is the second book I've written. Am I bragging? Heavens no. It seems I've been destined to write from day one. Just as I've been destined to fish my whole life.

Even as a child I was never an A student. Fact of the matter is, I would have been happy to be a C student. Actually the highest GPA I every attained was as a senior in high school, a 3.5. Did I mention that my subjects were social studies, gym, metal working III, woodworking III, and printing II?

What I'm saying up front is that I'm not the most intelligent guy on this planet. Fortunately for me I've compensated for the intelligence through lots of hard work and many, many years of life experiences. I don't give up easily. I've always lived by many philosophies, such as the words of my late father—"Put in a good eight hours of work every day and you will receive eight hours of pay." What the hell does that mean? "Work hard and you will be rewarded."

If it takes an above-average person one hour to learn something, it takes me eight hours. That's probably why I'm now in my sixties and writing a book on life experiences. It's taken me that long to really understand life. That may be a lot different from anyone else.

What makes me happy may not make someone else happy. It took me a long time for me to learn that simple statement. Remember, I'm a slow learner.

Many of my accomplishments came from sheer intestinal fortitude; that is, guts. Not talent, like the time I whitewater rafted over a sixteen foot waterfall and up a ten foot wall of water, or the several times I did the polar plunge— jumping into a lake in January in Wisconsin when the air temp is -10 and the water temp is 33°. Fact of the matter is, I think that confirms my level of intelligence, as did getting married at eighteen and having two children before the age of twenty. (By the way, I'm still married to the same woman after forty-five years.) Or attending each and every school function of all three of my children all the way through high school, or completing two full marathons (26.2 miles), and three half marathons without much training. It was sheer willpower.

Again I don't mention these things to brag but to tell you that although I may not have a lot of talent in any one area, I have survived in life by giving my all to everything I attempted.

Am I talented enough to be a well-known author? Time will tell. It's most important for you to understand that the information in this book is my perspective on fishing and life in general. If in some small way that helps you cope with the many curves life throws at us, then I will have accomplished one of my many goals in life.

This book was written over a four-year period. Almost all of its contents came to me while on the water or in the shower, unlike some of the greatest authors in the world who seem to have a constant flow of original ideas. As I mentioned, I'm not the smartest man on earth. It just takes me longer to learn.

I have been fishing for over sixty years and was just recently considered one of the better captains in our area. I worked in a profession for thirty years before I really became proficient. (That's another book.) I hope that each and every one of you will enjoy the story of a young boy obsessed with fishing who made a little dent in the world to become the man he is today.

My wish when I die is that people say about me what they said about my father, who died way too young. At his funeral, if I heard it once, I heard it a hundred times: "He sure was a nice guy." May my headstone not say He Lived to Fish but read" He Sure Was a Nice Guy"

Please enjoy my story.

# ACKNOWLEDGMENTS

To my bride of forty-five years: "Sister." Thank you for helping me develop my passion for fishing and putting up with me all these years. "Well, Sister …"

To my dad. If not for him, I never would have had a chance to have a LIW—"Line in the Water".

To my incredible, happy, healthy children, for without them my life would not be complete.

To Brady, one of my grandsons, for he humbles me every waking moment. He has accomplished so much in the short eighteen years that God has blessed us with his presence. Thank you, Brady. Yup!

Your husband, your son, your father and grandfather.

# CHAPTER 1

# THE EARLY YEARS

It all started when I was three years old. We lived two blocks from the "Little Lake" located in a small town in Wisconsin. The lake really wasn't that small. As a matter of fact, the lake was part of the Fox River, which flowed from Lake Winnebago to the bay of Green Bay, which is four hundred feet in elevation from Winnebago to the bay. What makes the lake so unusual is that Fox River flows north, just like the Nile River and the Red River in Minnesota. It defies all the laws of nature in North America. Maybe that's why the good Lord put the little lake two blocks from our house. Not too far away was a boat rental/bait shop that rented boats, motors, life jackets, worms, hellgrammites (a dragonfly larvae that is very good bait for perch). The bait shop was owned by the Fahenkrugs. I'm not sure where the owner worked full-time, but the missus always seemed to take care of things when we went there. Boats were $3.00 a day to rent, and the rental of an outboard motor was $5.00 a day. I don't recall how much worms were, as we always dug our own. We would buy minnows, but usually only three or six. The cost, to my recollection, was fifteen cents for three or twenty-five cents for six. When purchasing minnows, the missus always gave us what we ordered. If you ordered six, you got six. If you ordered a dozen minnows, you got twelve. Not eleven, not thirteen, but twelve. What made that so unique was many other bait shop in the area would always give you a couple more minnows for good measure. The bait shop was so close to our home and the only rental/bait place on the lake, so people patronized them for convenience.

## CHAPTER 2

# THINGS NEVER
# REALLY CHANGE

My first time fishing, to my best recollection, was with my dad when I was three years old. We rented a boat from the Fahenkrugs. "No motor," Dad said. It was too much money. He could row, and row he did. You see, even at that early age I learned that you always needed to fish on the other side of the lake in order to catch fish. Nobody ever fished on the side of the lake where they lived or where they launched their boat. It's always the other side of the lake. I remember asking my dad why we didn't just row out hundred yards from the rental dock and fish. He reminded me that the good fishing was on the other side of the lake by the red barn. I always noticed there were boats in front of the rental place fishing, but I guess they must have been from the other side of the lake. You know, fifty years later, I realized Dad was right. We still fish on the other side of the lake, no matter what lake we fish. God must have designed it that way, as I'm sure it was like that one hundred years ago and will be like that one hundred years from now.

How many times have you rented a cottage on a lake for a summer vacation, gone to the other side of the lake to fish, and come back empty-handed? No fish. And then the person who stayed at the cabin to read tells you that someone fishing right off the dock caught the biggest fish they had ever seen! Of course, you ask what kind of fish? What were they using for bait? What time was it? The person who stayed behind doesn't have a clue. So the next day you go across the lake again in the hopes of finding the big one. That's the way it was back then and still goes on today and will continue for many years to come.

Not too long ago a group of us went to Canada for our annual fishing trip (two grandkids, my sister, a nephew, and four friends). We were trying a new resort. Once we settled in, we went to meet with the owner of the resort to get information on where to fish. You guessed it. He said: "Lot of guys fish right out front of the resort and seem to catch little ones. If want bigger fish, look across the lake, three miles away, between the two big pines in eight to ten feet of water. You'll find the big ones."

We did go across the lake and we did catch fish, but after two days of boating three miles across the lake, we decided to try out front, a hundred yards out. We got big ones there also! Did I mention the owner also sells gas for the boats right at the resort?

I always wondered why the good Lord decided to put all the big fish on the other side of the lake between two big trees. I think he was answering the prayers of those that sold gas.

# CHAPTER 3

# MY MENTOR

My dad was from a very poor family. His mother raised seventeen children. How? We don't know. She was able to feed and clothe them all. I suspect my dad learned to fish for two reasons: (1) to help support the family and provide food for them, and (2) to get away from all the everyday chaos he grew up with. At age fourteen, all the kids in his family were expected to find work. I believe fishing was his sanctuary for at least a little while every so often. After he married his childhood sweetheart, who happened to be his first cousin (which might explain a lot about me) he had a couple of children and moved from the Upper Peninsula of Michigan to Wisconsin. You see, he worked two jobs, six days a week. I remember that every Sunday in the summer Dad would go fishing and I would go along. I don't remember any of my five sisters fishing with us, but one must have. How else would she have grown up to be a fisherman? At age sixty-eight she still enjoys fishing and fishes every day she can. She lives on a little lake. Not the little lake we grew up on but a small lake nonetheless. It is always funny how history repeats itself way too many times in our lives. By the way, three out of four of her children have a passion for fishing.

So it's another Sunday, and Dad and I go fishing. I couldn't sleep the night before. I should have known then that my passion in life was going to be fishing. We rented a fourteen foot boat. We brought some worms that dad had dug in the garden and rowed to the other side of the lake by the red barn. We were fishing for perch. I don't remember catching any perch on my first trip but I remember Dad getting a whole pail full. While on the boat I played with the anchor rope and reeled in my pole about a hundred times, but I didn't want to touch any worms. And most important, I wasn't going to touch the fish in the pail. It really wasn't all about catching fish or fishing back then. It was being with my dad. He never said much, but led by example. More on that subject later. But could it be that at the age of three or four I already knew what fishing was really all about? We will see.

Dad always worked from 3 p.m. to 11 p.m. Monday through Friday at the local paper mill. He drove a tow motor, but his passion in life seemed to be that of a mason/carpenter. I guess he was smart enough to know that back then, in the fifties, the mill provided job security, health insurance, and a weekly paycheck. On mornings from 8 a.m. to noon and on Saturdays he would do his mason work. He had several friends in the mill that built homes part-time. Some of them hired him to build chimneys or pour concrete for sidewalks and driveways. The work not only allowed him to develop his passion, but he also put a little extra money on the table to pay bills. Looking back at it, I realize Dad would probably have done all the mason work for free just so he'd have the challenge of figuring out how to build a chimney or pour a driveway. He never said it but he knew that when you find your passion in life, it really isn't work and it makes very little difference how much money you earn.

Dad had little formal education. He went to the school of hard knocks starting at age fourteen, yet he was an accomplished mason, carpenter, musician, and quite a good fisherman. I guess building, concrete work, and learning how to play six or seven different musical instruments allowed him to become a patient and understanding man. The patience came in handy when Dad took me out fishing on those Sundays, because like most four year olds I played more than I fished. As time went by, I learned from my dad how to fish and how to wait for the fish to bite. Dad did a great job teaching by example, as he was a man of few words.

## Chapter 4

# First Fishing Partner

My love for fishing was shared by my first cousin Pat. We were the same age and lived seven houses apart. I don't recall Pat fishing with my dad and me, but when we were about six or seven, Pat and I would walk down to the lake and fish. I think we fished every day in the summer, and every Saturday and Sunday during the school year. We would dig worms and buy three minnows, and then fish off the dock for perch and northern pike. It seems we always caught a couple, and sometimes even ten or fifteen. We always split them up; I would bring home half and Pat would bring home half.

I'm not sure our parents were so appreciative of our catch. You see, my family had six kids, and our grandmother lived with us. Pat's family consisted of eight boys. When I brought home, say, three seven-inch perch, my mom would always say, "Dale, we will clean these up so we can have them for supper." It seems to me we did have fish fries, but Mom must have frozen all the smaller batches of fish until there was enough to feed us all. Boy, parents sure were smart back then. Or was it survival instinct, figuring out how to feed a large family on so little money? Either way, Mom never told me not to bring fish home no matter how many I brought.

Even at that age I would go to bed and not be able to fall asleep because I was thinking about fishing the next day. Not too many years ago a nephew of mine asked, "How do you develop a passion?" Well, I don't know that I had an answer. Our passion can be anything we're exposed to. No matter how hard or easy it is, it is never work but a passion.

Not too long ago that nephew found his passion after fifty years on earth. Now he sometimes has trouble going to sleep at night, thinking about how to build his next project. It might be a table or a birdhouse. At the end of the day he says the same thing most people say when have found their passion: "I cannot believe I've been out working on my project for five hours. It seems I just got started."

Good for him!

## CHAPTER 5

# THE LONG WALK HOME

Times were a little different back in the fifties. At only seven years old, Pat and I would be by alone at the lake and our parents knew it. They just told us to be home by lunch. One time Pat and I went to the little lake to fish for perch. We always fished off the bait shop's dock. This time Pat had to be home early, so I stayed after he left. Why would I give up a day of fishing just because no one else was there to fish with? I think that is when I started enjoying fishing by myself. I'm not sure if it is the solitude or not having to talk to anyone or that I could just daydream and let my mind wander.

While I was there fishing by myself, I decided that maybe the fish would be biting better a couple of docks farther down the lake. I was right! I caught a stringer of perch. More perch than I'd ever caught in my life at the time. The problem came when I was supposed to be home for lunch. I didn't even think of lunch because I was catching fish. Of course, what I didn't know was Mom wasn't so concerned about me eating lunch as she was about knowing where I was and if I was okay. When I wasn't home by noon, she sent down my older sister Lois to find me. At that time, I don't think Lois liked me too much. Some brothers and sisters seem to hate each other when they are young, and then as life goes on, they mature and become best friends. That is what happened with Lois and me. Anyhow, Lois came down to look for me. She went right to the bait shop's dock. Like any other twelve-year-old, when she didn't see me there, she didn't bother to look any further. She went home and told our mom that I wasn't on the dock where I always was.

I'm not sure what time it was when I finally made it home. Later I was told it was 4 p.m. I had twenty-seven perch, and all big ones. For a seven-year-old, big could be five inches long. I was still on the dock, and the next thing I know a police officer was talking to me. He asked my name and said my mom was looking for me and he would bring me home. When I got home, I was so excited to show everyone my twenty-seven fish. When my mom opened the door, she saw the police officer but not me, and she started to cry. I had been standing behind the officer because I wanted to surprise her with my stringer of perch. When she saw me, she seemed to be mad but was crying and hugging me. I thought maybe she was excited about my fish!

I learned later that Mom thought I had fallen in the water and drowned. I was too young to understand her feeling until later in life, when I had children. When I thought of how my mom must have felt … That poor woman. Of course I was told that I could *never* go to the lake again by myself. Maybe that's another reason I fish by myself because I was told to never fish again by myself. Wow, that's kind of deep psychological profiling. (Mom loved us all.)

# CHAPTER 6

# TIME TO TEACH OTHERS

My wife and I have three children of our own, one boy and two girls. There were countless times when one of our kids was supposed to be home at a certain time and wasn't. And there were times when they were supposed to be at someone's home but weren't. When they did not come home on time we called the other house and they weren't there ... Your heart stops. What happened to them? Are they all right?

When they finally come home we tell them they are never going over to so-and-so's house again and that they are grounded for life ... and then two days later the same thing happens and we start all over again! No, things do not really change from generation to generation. We human beings have short memories.

That reminds me of the priest giving the sermon at our church many years back on Easter Sunday: "I welcome all of you today and hope that it will not take another year for some of you to come back to church. We all know it is important to practice our religion every day and to pray to God so that he gives us guidance to do the right thing. But as we all know, sometimes we make mistakes. We ask for forgiveness and say that we will never do that again."

He then said, "Let me tell you a little story that happened to me. Not too long ago I was driving my little sports car down a country road when I said to myself, I wonder how fast this thing will go. I looked down at the speedometer. It read 105 mph. Just then I lost control of the car and was heading for a large tree. I prayed, 'Lord, if you let me live after this crash, I will never speed again.' Next thing I know I'm stopped in an open field and I'm not hurt. My car is trashed but not me. I got down on my knees and thanked God for letting me survive the crash and swore I would never again do something so foolish. Two months later I'm driving my new sports car down a back road enjoying the day when I say to myself, I wonder how fast this new one will go.…"

Yes, we all have the same short memories and maybe that's a good thing.

# CHAPTER 7

# MY GUARDIAN ANGEL

I was drawn to water no matter where I was. For two weeks of every year my parents sent me up to the Upper Peninsula to stay with my cousin Ernie. Even though my aunt and uncle and cousins didn't live on a lake or near a lake, we always seemed to find a creek or pond to fish. We would catch frogs and use them as bait for northern pike. All I wanted to do was fish. Was it an Obsession or passion? Is it the same? It is always interesting how things seem to make more sense later on in life than they do when you're going through it.

I'll divert a little. When I read Mitch Albom's book, *The Five People You Meet in Heaven*, I wondered if there was some truth to the idea that certain events occur at certain times for a reason. An example:

I was eight years old and, as usual, I was at the lake. I had received permission from the bait shop owner to fish off his dock. It was May and this bait shop also rented out fishing boats. At that time of year some of the boats were stacked up on the dock, leaning up against one another and leaving just enough room for an eight-year-old to fish off the dock. I had enough room to put my minnow can and pole on the dock. I was by myself, as usual, fishing for northern pike with my cane—that is, bamboo—pole. (A bamboo pole can be anywhere from eight feet to sixteen feet long. The longer, the better, as you could fish farther away from the dock or boat.) Apparently the serious of events that followed were unexplainable.

A gust of wind came up and knocked down one of the boats that was stacked on the dock. It hit me. I fell in the water; it was about five to six feet deep. I did not know how to swim. I can still to this day see what it was like to be underwater and drowning. Can't breathe … see bubbles … fighting to get to the top of the water … and then nothing. All went black. The next thing I remember, I was on the shore. Some young guy was kneeling next to me, asking if I was okay. Then a small group of people surrounded me. A police officer asked me my name. Was I destined to be always talking to police officers? And what had happened?

I told the officer that I fell in the water and that a young man jumped in and saved my life. The officer asked, "What young man?" I looked around and didn't see him. The other people there said they couldn't recall where that fellow went.

I believe even now that I died that day, but apparently the big guy felt I need to be around for many years. For what reason, I don't know yet. Maybe somehow touch other people's lives, or maybe to teach so many people how enjoyable fishing truly can be, or teach people how fishing can and will change your life. I'll touch on all of those areas later in this book.

The policeman took me home to my parents again. Mom wasn't crying when we got there, but after the officer explained what happened, she hugged me and kept crying.

Of course, after that near-death experience I was told, "You can never go to the lake again by yourself." Yes, Mom. Two days later, there I was again at the lake with Cousin Pat....

I wish I could say that when I was drowning I saw God or some deceased grandparents, but I have recollection of seeing the light that everyone talks about. So life went on as usual—fish, school, fish, and fish some more.

CHAPTER 8

# THE FROZEN TUNDRA

My obsession for fresh-water fishing did not end when the weather turned cold. The lake would freeze over with anywhere from six to twenty-four inches of ice. It was then time for ice fishing. The lake would freeze from the surface down when the water temperature dropped below 32° Fahrenheit. In twenty-four hours it could make one to two inches of ice. The lake would freeze over around mid-November and stay frozen until late March. We would take an ice chisel—a flat piece of iron six inches long and two inches wide welded to a long round pipe—and would chop a hole in the ice about six inches around. Lots of work, but work hard and you will be rewarded. At least that's what they would say.

Did you ever wonder who *they* are? *They* seem to have a world of knowledge. At least in the Midwest you would hear people say: they say it is going to rain: they say that driving too fast causes accidents; they say if you drink too much it kills brain cells (this one I've witnessed many times); they say if you fish too much, you will grow gills. It seems to go on and on. To this day, I still have not met the "*they*" person or people. Guess I never will. They say that it will drive you crazy to keep wondering who *they* are. They say it causes you to keep repeating yourself if think too much about it. I said, they say it causes you to keep repeating yourself if you …

Back to how ice fishing works.

After we chopped our holes in the ice, which sometimes would take half an hour to an hour, we would take our homemade jigging fishing poles, which consisted of a wire coat hanger straightened out with a bend at the end to make an eye. The other end would go into a wooden block about six inches long and one inch square. We would then put black thirty-pound fishing line on the pole, about six feet of line, and attach a fishing hook to it. Bait was chicken fat that Mom saved from the chicken she'd bought on Saturday for our Sunday night dinner.

We would take our poles, bait, and a wooden crate Dad made for us to sit on, and walk onto the frozen lake. We were not allowed to go on the lake unless there was at least six inches of ice. I'm not sure how Mom or Dad knew when there was the required six inches of ice, but I suspect Dad would check on us so we could sit and fish all day. Sometimes we caught none, some days we caught a few, and some days we caught our limit.

You know, it appears that fishing has not changed much in sixty years. We still some days catch nothing and other days many. That's why they call it fishing. See, they even know about fishing. (The first thing I'm going to do when I leave these earthly fishing grounds and arrive at the pearly gates, I'm to ask St. Peter who in the heck was that they person.)

Weather in Wisconsin in the winter can be quite challenging, with temperatures that can drop from 30°-40° to -25°.It could be windy or calm, snow, snow, or more snow. Whatever the weather we sat out on the ice and fished with our backs to the wind. Dad would always say it kept us warmer without the wind in our faces. Our hands would get so cold we had no feeling in our fingers. Some days I would hope I didn't catch a fish so I wouldn't have to take off my woolen mittens.

Where did we get our woolen mittens you ask? Well, I had two grandmas while growing up. My dad's mother was a knitter. She would knit each and every grandchild either a pair of wool mittens or a pair of wool socks. At one point she had over one hundred grand and great-grandchildren. Grandma was poorer than anyone I knew. So how was she able to make so many socks and mittens? She would go to Goodwill and buy old wool sweaters for five cents, pull them apart, and then rewind them into a ball of yarn. Now that was recycling long before the term *recycling* came about. So that's how I got my wool mittens.

# CHAPTER 9

# HOW POOR WERE WE?

I come from a lower to middle-class family, and it seems most of the people we knew had the same meals all the time. I don't recall Monday through Friday, but on Saturday we had cereal for breakfast, hot dogs for lunch, and supper was homemade biscuits and pancakes. Yes, pancakes. It was a very cheap meal. For a Saturday night snack … popcorn. Sunday lunch was chicken, mashed potatoes, and a vegetable. I'm not sure what Sunday night's meal was, but I would guess leftovers. We always had leftovers. Mom must have been cooking all the time. How a family of nine even had leftovers, I will never understand. Or how our parents had enough money to buy groceries and pay bills. In 1967 Dad made $2.20 an hour working in the mill. He had a part-time job that paid twice that amount. We had many easy and cheap meals, so the big meal on Sunday was always a treat. And, of course, we always had dessert. We had Chocolate pie, or brownies, or our favorite by far, chocolate cake with peanut butter frosting. To this day every year on my birthday my wife makes chocolate cake with peanut butter frosting. Thanks, Mom, for introducing us to that incredible cake.

I look back now and think that my parents really did appreciate all the fish I brought home. A free meal, as they say. And there *they* are again!

Our family of nine consisted of six kids, my parents, and my grandmother all living in a two-bedroom house. I slept in the same room as Grandma, the girls slept in another room, and Mom and Dad and my brother Ricky were in another room. (I'll talk later about Ricky.)

My dad worked in the paper mill driving a tow motor, a lift truck that he used to move pallets of paper from one location to another. Dad always worked the 3 p.m. to 11 p.m. shift. On Saturdays he did his part-time job as a mason/carpenter. He could build anything, which was amazing considering he only completed the eighth grade and then went to work like many of his brothers and sisters. It was even amazing that Dad worked in the mill at all. You see, from when he was fourteen until he was thirty-five, Dad worked as a lumberjack and then did a lot of farm work. Basically, he took any type of work that was done outdoors. To work indoors must have been plain hell for him. It was good pay, though, and as Mom always preached, he had job security and health insurance.

Thank God Mom and Dad had health insurance. You see, my brother Ricky was born with some major health issues and was not expected to live beyond one year. He beat the odds and lived at home until age nineteen. I'll tell a lot more about Ricky at a later time.

CHAPTER **10**

# KIDS WILL BE KIDS

Wait a second. I thought fishing was about catching fish. Is it possible my passion in life is fishing and not catching fish?

I guess I learned at a young age that fishing really wasn't about catching fish as much as all the other things that go along with it. Making friends, being alone, enjoying the outdoors, breathing healthy air, mentoring, making others happy, sharing experiences, learning, talking with loved ones, learning about weather, overcome adversity, enjoy God's wonders.

As a matter of fact, I never thought much about what an impact, fishing had on all my children. Let me tell you one of many rewarding, heartwarming stories about my son. Not too long ago he and I were talking about his divorce, which had happened eighteen years earlier. He told me that if I had not taken him to Canada the summer of his divorce, he wasn't sure what kind of foolish thing he would have done. When I asked what he meant, he explained that he and his wife were fighting constantly and he was afraid he might lose his temper and do something he regretted. We were in Canada for ten days, and during that time we talked about everything that came to mind. Finally he vented to me about his marital problems. We talked for days on end and he came up with a game plan. The marriage couldn't be saved, but both he and his ex-wife moved on and became much happier. Who would have thought that a fishing trip could actually be a therapeutic session and help restructure a person's life?

## CHAPTER 11

# A MOTHER IS ALWAYS THERE

When I would bring fish home, Mom and I would have to wait for Dad to get home to clean the fish. I'm not sure if I didn't do a good job cleaning fish or that since I was only six or so, my parents didn't feel comfortable having me use a knife that could easily cut a finger off. Dad always said, "The only way to eat fish is with the bones in the fish." I was told it gave it better flavor. So we would scale the fish first in the kitchen. Needless to say, scales always seemed to go flying everywhere. We had scales all over dishes, cupboards, and even in the dog dish. Then Dad would cut the heads off and take out the insides, a process known as gutting the fish. Sometimes when we gutted the fish, its belly would be full of spawn (fish eggs). Most of the time they would still be in the spawn sack, kind of like onions in a bag. Dad would keep those eggs and then put them back in with the cleaned fish.

Mom would always fry up the fish in a pan of lard, but also she would fry up the fish eggs for us kids. We were told they tasted just like the fish except there were no bones. Later on, I did the same with our kids. I also realized my parents were making ends meet, stretching whatever food we had to make it last. But you know, the fish eggs were quite good. Many people pay big dollars for fish eggs when they're called caviar and we got them for free!

## Chapter 12

# Who Needs Money to Build an Ice Shanty?

Sitting on the ice and getting cold. Some of the old-timers made wind blocks out of cardboard, which consisted of a three-by-four-foot piece of cardboard attached to two 2 x 4s. They would chop two small holes in the ice and put the 2 x 4s in the holes and cover them with ice and water. In a couple minutes, the wind break was stationary. The old-timers would sit behind their wind shields to stay warm. It was actually about twenty degrees warmer out of the wind, or at least it seemed that way.

As I got older, in the 1950's, some old-timers actually built a small house out of wood to sit in on the ice. It was maybe four feet by four feet and six feet high, with a small door. It had two holes drilled through the floor, so you could slide your house over the holes you'd chopped in the ice and fish completely out of the wind, snow, or whatever else Mother Nature threw at you. These little houses were called shanties.

My cousin Pat and I came up with a great ice fishing hut. Up town, six blocks from our home was an appliance store that sold refrigerators, kitchen stoves, TVs, etc. The appliance store was across from the local theater, which was called the Brin Theater. Back in the '50s, all the big appliances came in cardboard boxes not just regular size boxes but *big* boxes. Pat said to me one day when we were on the way to the Brin theater to see *The Lone Ranger*, wouldn't those big boxes make a great shanty? Wow. What a great idea, I thought. But where would we get the money to buy one of these great shanties for two people? Pat and I had shoveled for the neighbors after every snowfall. We made twenty-five cents for sidewalks and fifty cents for a whole driveway. If only our parents had taught us to save some of that money. We always spent it on candy or a show as soon as we made it.

As luck would have it, we stopped at the appliance store one day right after a delivery was made and asked if we could have one of the large boxes. We explained what we were going to do with it and the owner told us to take it. So we got our first shanty for free. We had to try it out right away, so we took it down to the lake to set it up. In our excitement, we forgot to pick up our fishing gear. We had to decide who was going back home to get the poles, bait, and ice chisel and who would stay with our shanty. Pat, as usual, talked me into going back to get the gear. He always seemed to talk me into something. I ran home as fast as I could, filled with excitement. I got our gear and was running back to the lake when I met

Pat coming towards me. He was crying, just as I would be five minutes later.

It seems Pat thought he would try out our new shanty by himself. He stood on the ice and put the large box over him, and of course it became very dark. Since he couldn't see, he quickly pushed the box off him as hard as he could. The box went flying, and the wind blew our brand-new shanty all the way across the lake. I started to cry, too, and headed for home with Pat. Once in I was in my house, Mom asked me what happened. I told her the story. She looked as sad as I felt, but I now know deep down she was trying not to laugh. Parents have been blessed with the ability to say the right thing at the right time for their children, as I learned many years later.

Mom said she would talk to Dad when he got home and see if he had any ideas. Boy, did he come up with some ideas. I don't know how Dad got so smart. Like that famous Mark Twain quote: "When I was fourteen, my father was so ignorant I could hardly stand to have the old man around. But when I got to be twenty-one, I was astonished at how much the old man had learned in seven years." But when it came to building things, Dad sure knew how to do it. He took a Sunday afternoon and built us a real shanty out of scrap wood. It even had a door and a window and was big enough for four people. At least it looked that big compared to our little cardboard one. It turned out it was big enough for four people, if two of them were kids.

It was late when he finished, but Pat and I talked Dad into dragging our new shanty down to the lake to get it in position. We got it on the shoreline of ice and left it there until we could get it to the exact right spot in the daylight. Now think about it. Finding the right spot on a lake one mile wide and two miles long? What would be the right spot? Actually, there is some logic to it. If you caught fish in the summer in one area, chances were you would catch them there in the winter.

After school the next day Pat and I ran down to the lake and slid our shanty to the exact spot we wanted. We thought as long as we were there, we might as well fish. Surprise! We'd been so excited to move our shanty that we forgot our poles and an ice chisel. The next three days brought so much cold and snow we were unable to even go on the lake. It was all we thought and talked about. As we walked to our Catholic school in the morning, we guessed how many fish we would catch in our new shanty.

CHAPTER 13

# POEM WRITING AT ITS BEST

While at school that week, Sister "Better-do-it-right-or-else" Mary advised us that we needed to write a poem for homework. She gave us four days to write the poem, and then on Friday she would select the best poem and that person would read it *in front of the class.* Who in God's name would want to write a poem so good that they would have to read it aloud to the class? Pat and I agreed to work together and write the worst poem we could, to prevent either of us from going in front of the class.

Our first question was what subject we should use for our poem that was guaranteed to fail. I guess it took us all of a minute to come up with our subject—the shanty. Well, we worked two days nonstop. Okay, we worked on it for five minutes, but for an eight-year-old, it felt like two days. After all that time, those five minutes, we had nothing. So we decided to sleep on the matter, but then inspiration struck. We'd take a well-known poem and just change the words a little. Sure would save us a lot of time, and it surely wouldn't be good enough to win. The poem we were studying in school that week was "My Shadow" by Robert Louis Stevenson.

> I have a little shadow that goes in and out of me.
> And what can be the use of him is more than I can see.
> He is very, very like me from the heels up to the head;
> And I see him jump before me, when I jump into my bed.
>
> The funniest thing about him is the way he likes to grow—

Not at all like normal people, which is,
always very slow;
For he sometimes shoots up tall like an
red-rubber ball,
And sometimes so small, that there's
none of him at all.

All we had to do was change a couple of
words and the poem would be ours, and we
would be sure to not win!

Our Shanty by Pat and Dale

I have a little shanty that was built for
Pat and me.
What kind of fish can we catch in there
is hard to believe.
It was made by my dad for four people to
use on the ice
But it turns out it is only big enough for
two adults and two kids no bigger than
a mice.

The nicest thing about it is the swinging door and window.

Not like the one in a house but this one actually is one that was bought at a store.

It sometimes keeps us very warm and snug

And sometimes it is so cold that we need to cover up with a rug!

We figured this had to be the worst poem ever written, and for sure we didn't have to worry about Sister "Better-do-it-right-or-else" Mary selecting our poem as the best.

Well, Friday came, and Sister Mary said she would finish reading all the poems after lunch and announce the winner, and would Pat and Dale please stay when everyone else went to lunch. What did we do? No other kids around, just Sister and us. We figured we'd never see our friends again. Good-bye, world. What were we going to tell our parents when we got kicked out of school?

So Pat and I were alone in the classroom. Sister Mary looked at us as only a nun could and said, "Well, boys, we have a problem." I didn't know why she said *we*. For sure, she didn't have a problem, Pat and I did! "I've read your poem and well, I'm a little confused. Did you boys come up with this poem all by yourself?"

If you've ever had a nun for a teacher, then you know they all went to the police academy to learn how to interview a suspect, and for some reason they always knew when you were lying. We had to try anyway. "Yes, Sister, this is our idea. Pretty good, eh?" We laughed.

We were not very smart because two things you never do in front of a nun are lie and laugh. It was all downhill from there. She proceeded to tell us it was a sin to lie, and if we kept lying we would go right to hell. And since we thought this was so funny, maybe we should share with the class what exactly was funny. We tried to speak, but all we got was "Keep your mouths shut and listen." Blah, blah, blah, and for copying another person's poem you both get an F for the assignment, and also, as punishment you will both read your poem in front of the class and then tell everyone you stole the poem from someone else.

But, but, but …

"No buts!" she said. "Right after lunch you will read that stolen poem."

Wow. First we were going to hell, and even worse, we had to read in front of the class. We both agreed we would rather be in hell than in front of the class.

She dismissed us and told us to join our class in the cafeteria. On the way there, Pat and I knew all the kids would ask what happened. So we came up with a great plan. We got our trays and lunch and sat down with our class of eighteen students.

Sally, the know-it-all teacher's pet who everyone hated, said, "Well, Pat and Dale, what did you do this time?" Like we'd been in trouble before … But that's another story.)

Then why did Sister Mary keep you after class? To give you an award?

Well, Sally, that's none of your business, I said, but you're going to find out soon enough. All I'm going to say is Sister Mary asked us to recite our poem in front of the class and—

*What?* You guys won the poem contest? That can't be. I know I had the best. You're lying, aren't you?

Pat and I didn't say a word as she started crying. We just smiled.

By the time we were done reading our poem out loud in front of the class, all the kids were crying. The kids were crying from laughter that is. After everyone settled down, Sister Mary told us to explain were we got our ideas from. We had to admit that we stole the idea from Robert Louis Stevenson and we would probably go right to hell for doing so. Just as we sat down who walks in our class but Father Maas. It was like he always knew when someone was doing something bad.

Just stopped in to wish you all a nice weekend, he began. Yes, Sister? Talk in private? Sure.

Oh, boy. Not only were we going to hell, but we were going right now.

Well, class, Father Maas said, Sister Blabbermouth tells me we have a couple of young boys in class today that did something very wrong, but you know, God forgives everyone, even bad sinners. So I'm sure that if these two fellows promise the Lord that they will never do what they did every again, God will forgive them.

Father, does this mean we're not going to hell?

Well, boys, not today, that's for sure.

Priests, like parents, always seem to know what to say at the right time to make you feel better. As for Sister Mary, if eyes could kill … She was not too happy with Father Maas's approach. I think she really wanted us to go to hell!

The winter came and went, and yes we did get to use our new shanty, but after the poem fiasco, the shanty was never the same. It was like Sister Mary had jinxed our Shanty. We never really caught a lot of fish out of that shanty.

# CHAPTER 14

# MY BROTHER

My obsession with fishing continued. I talked fishing, wrote about fishing, made fishing poles, and made fishing lures. I even had fish pajamas my mom sewed for me. Mom seemed to always be sewing something. I found out later in life that it was because we couldn't afford a lot of new things. Mom would have gladly done odd jobs if she could, but her full-time job was raising us kids and taking care of my brother Ricky. Ricky was physically and mentally handicapped. He had hydrocephalus, a condition in which there is too much fluid around the brain. Back in 1953 when he was born, the doctors did not know how to help someone like him, so the fluid kept accumulating and his head got bigger and bigger, compressing the brain. He was not expected to live beyond nine months old, but for some reason, the good Lord kept him around for nineteen years. Ricky was doing pretty well until age four. He could walk and say a few words, but then he lost his sight when he was four. From that point on he was very much like a one- or two-year-old. His body kept growing but his mind didn't. He became bedridden as he was too hard to handle. He stayed in Mom and Dad's bedroom. Even though he couldn't talk, he was my buddy. I would say good-bye in the morning and come into see him after school, and we would talk. He would laugh. I'm not sure if he understood me, but I do know he knew I was there.

In those early years I don't remember going out to a restaurant with my parents or sisters. I'm not sure if it was the money or that it was too hard to bring Ricky. Guess I'll never know.

Many stories arise because of Ricky. He touched each and every person who knew him. Maybe that is why he was around for so long. I'll talk more about Ricky later. As my mom always said" There is a good reason for everything that happens to us in life."

## Chapter 15

# The Maynards

Pat and I fished just about every day for as long as I can remember. He had six other brothers and no sisters. His mom was my dad's sister and his last name was Maynard. The Maynards and my family were close. I ate at the Maynards', slept at the Maynards', and if some of the boys got punished and I was there, I got punished also. I'm not sure if Pat's parents got confused and thought they had eight boys. I was there more than I was at home. Boots—my aunt's nickname—always set a plate for me. I think when I wasn't there, she would set out a plate, and when everyone sat down to eat and I wasn't there, I'm sure she said, "Where's Dale?" The boys would laugh and she would realize I wasn't one of hers.

If Boots punished me, it's because my mom would say, if he does something wrong, take care of it. And that she did. I never really knew my uncle Wally that well. Seems he worked a lot.

Pat was six months older than I, so for a while, when I was nine, Pat was ten. I only remember bits and pieces of that day, but I did know my life would never be the same.

"What do you mean I can't go to Pat's today? I always go to Pat's. Where did his dad go? He's gone? Gone where? I'm going to Pat's. Pat's crying. Why? The boys are crying and Boots told me I should go home. Why?"

Wally was forty-two years old, a mill worker with seven boys all at home and a spouse who didn't work, who did not even drive a car. Wally Sr. had a massive heart attack. He was gone before he hit the ground.

"What does that mean? When is he coming home? Why is Pat crying and he doesn't want to see me?" I had asked.

Wally was gone. Little did I know that my best friend, my fishing buddy, and my *teachers*, the Maynards, they would soon be leaving the neighborhood. I don't remember the funeral, and I don't know if I went or not. All I know is Pat was never the same for a long time after that day. He always seemed to be mad. That spring he told me that they were moving to Combined Locks some ten miles away, to a new house. Why Boots picked that area or why they moved at all, I still do not know to this day. Though it was only ten miles, it might as well have been 1,000 miles. I couldn't walk there. I couldn't ride my bike there. But most of all, who could I go fishing with?

"Dale," my mom said, "you can go visit Pat once in a while. I'll bring you out there when I can."

It didn't happen often. When I did get to stay at Pat's, there was no place to fish, just to build tree houses and forts in the woods, a new experience for a city boy. And then there were girls. Not just girls, but young women. At least to a ten-year-old, girls who were twelve or fourteen seemed like young women. Well, that is another whole book in itself. Let's just say Pat was over fishing and had replaced it with girls. I wasn't ready to give up fishing yet.

Now that I look back, I guess that's when I learned to enjoy fishing by myself. To this day, as much as I enjoy the company of others while fishing, a day all alone on the ice or a boat is ever so relaxing. The only thing present was just the fish, the sky, the good Lord, and myself, and of course the spirit of Ricky. I had to fish for him since he never had a chance.

I fished that spring, summer, and winter by myself. Dad didn't fish on Sundays anymore.

## Chapter 16

# Dad Had It Good!

Dad was really fortunate the good Lord gave him so many things to deal with. He came from a family of seventeen children and a house with dirt floors. His father was thirty-nine when he died. My dad never finished eighth grade, but worked on a farm full-time for room and board when he was fourteen. He married his childhood sweetheart and had six children, one of whom was handicapped. He moved his family from the Upper Peninsula to Menasha, Wisconsin, and got a job in the mill, inside work that probably wasn't so comfortable for a farm boy/lumberjack. And he worked part-time as a self-taught mason/carpenter, but he never had a lot of money. So why was he so fortunate?

He had a dream and a goal. He was able to fulfill that dream, which was to buy a piece of land in the country and build a home on it with his own two hands. Where he got the money, I do not know, but my dad bought a piece of land in the country and he built a 1100 square foot home on that half acre parcel. I didn't fish much that year as I was always with Dad at the new home, helping mix mortar and hand boards and nails to him.

My dad must have helped an awful lot of people through the years, because every hour he was there working on the new home, some friend or relative would show up to help build Bert's dream. I guess they wanted him to enjoy his dream. In December 1959 we sold our house and moved to our new home seven miles out in the country.

Wow! I'm excited. Wait, are we near a lake? Mom, what am I going to do out there? I won't know anyone. I can't fish? Can you take me to the lake every weekend?

Dad lived his dream, something so few people ever do. I thought he'd given up on fishing. We didn't fish on Sundays that whole summer, but in June we were back to fishing. Not on every Sunday, though, only some. He didn't give up on fish. He just found something else he enjoyed more—his dream.

## CHAPTER 17

## FREE THERAPY

No fishing after school. No fishing on Saturday or Sunday. Now I was even farther away from Pat my cousin. Mom tried sending me up to the Upper Peninsula for couple weeks at a time that summer to stay with my cousins, the Haights. They had four boys and one girl, Mary Jo, who was my age Jim the oldest, Ernie four years older then myself Gil 4 years younger then myself, and the youngest Robbie. We had gone up there every summer and someone would stay, my sisters or me, for a week or so, and then the boys would come to the city and stay with us. We always had so much fun with Uncle Lloyd and Aunt Whitie. Whitie was my mother's sister and my dad's cousin. ( It is a long story. Let's just say our family tree has no limbs).

Mom thought it would be great therapy for me to spend time out in the middle of nowhere in a small town of four hundred people. As usual—parents are so smart—Mom was right. Mary Jo and I had a great time messing around, looking for chipmunks and climbing trees. My cousin Ernie was four years older than Mary Jo and myself, but we got along pretty well. He liked to hunt as much as I liked to fish. When he wasn't in school, he was hunting squirrel, rabbits, woodchucks, gophers, birds, whatever there was to hunt. But he also like to trout fish.

"Ernie," Aunt Whitie said one day, "take Dale trout fishing with you."

"Ma, he's not old enough. He'll scare all the fish. He doesn't have a pole and he's not using mine!"

Thank God Whitie won out and Ernie took me to a place he called crooked creek. I don't recall if I caught any brook trout, but Ernie got three nice ones. He told his mom I only caught chubs. At the time I didn't know the difference between a trout and chub, so for all I know I could have caught trout. I do know that I was hooked on trout fishing. The fish were smaller than some of the fish I caught in the little lake, but they seemed to fight harder. And you could see the fish bite. It was an unforgettable two weeks. We would go out at night with a flashlight and pick night crawlers for fishing the next day. Go fishing early before the flies and mosquitoes came out. Come home and then go back toward evening. At the time I wasn't sure which Ernie liked best, hunting or fishing. I would learn later in life that hunting was his passion.

Yes, moms always know the right thing to do.

## CHAPTER 18

# THE START OF A
# LIFETIME FRIENDSHIP

When I was invited up to my cousin, Ernie's place in the Upper Peninsula, he showed me how to trap squirrels and rabbits. Box traps for rabbits and rat traps—actually, spring traps—for squirrels. So of course as most kids, when I got back home I asked my dad if I could trap squirrels and rabbits in the woods behind our new country home. He agreed it would be a great idea and said he would help me build some box traps. I asked if he know how and found out later he got a good laugh out of that. He had been quite the trapper many years earlier, but when he moved to the city, he got away from it. He built me some box traps and I had one spring trap, and I spent most of the year trapping rabbits and squirrels. Like when I'd fished every day in the city, as soon as I came home from school I'd check my traps. I caught quite a few squirrels and learned to skin them. Mom would cook them up for an evening meal. I know she might have discarded the rabbits and cooked chicken instead, so I'm not sure if we actually ate rabbit.

Trapping was all I could think of. I couldn't fish, so I trapped. I did not make any neighborhood friends for the first year or so. I was pretty much a loner even back then. One day Mom (moms are so smart) asked me to go across the street to the Meyer farm and pick up some eggs she'd ordered. They had milk cows and chickens on the farm. Gibby and Florence were the farmers, and Florence sold eggs to all the neighbors.

The Meyers had three children. Bob, who was two years older than me, Dennis (three years younger), and Stevie (five years younger). I didn't want to go over to the Meyers that day but Mom made me go. Boy, parents can be mean, at least to a 12 year old. Apparently Mom had talked to Florence ahead of time and set it up so I could meet Bob.

I got there and Florence told me the eggs weren't ready. She had to wash them all. As a matter of fact, whenever anyone came to pick up eggs, they were never ready. Even if you called ahead to tell Florence you were coming, they would not be ready. I think it was her way of getting people to hang around and tell her information. She was the one in the neighborhood who knew everything. If you came home at three in the morning, she knew it. To this day I do not think she ever slept.

Florence told me while she was cleaning the eggs that I could go out to the barn and watch Bob feed the cows. I had never been inside a barn before and or even up close to a cow, so I jumped at the idea. Bob demonstrated how to feed the cows and showed me his favorite calf. You know how sometimes relationships click? Well, Bob and I became best friends on that day, and even now, some fifty-five years later, we see each other weekly. How can one man have so much good fortune in life?

Bob and I were like Pat and me. When I wasn't at home or school I was at Bob's. I ate there, I did chores there, I drove (or rode along) tractors, cleaned gutter (remove cow manure). We were inseparable. Then I met his friend Tiny. Tiny lived down the road a piece and had two older brothers. He lived with his dad, Ben, and their housekeeper Gertrude, or Gertie. Tiny's mom died young, but I'm not sure when or how.

We were like the Three Musketeers, having fun together, getting into trouble together. That winter I think I forgot about fishing until one day Gibby, Bob's dad, asked if I liked to fish. I couldn't believe my ears. Was he kidding, for he must know I fish?

I sure do, I answered. Why?

Well, after chores on Saturday, Bob and I go ice fishing for walleye and perch on Bago, the largest inland lake in Wisconsin. The lake was seven miles wide, twenty-five miles long.

Would I like to go? I asked. We could get up early and get chores done early so we could go. Gibby said he didn't think his milking cows would appreciate a change in schedule, but we could get some other things done a little earlier.

Oh my God, I'm in the country, no lake within eight miles, and I get to go ice fishing. There is a God!

After that we went fishing every Saturday and caught lots of fish. Bob and I had a great time. And we had no shanty. We sat outside or in Gibby's truck with a kerosene heater in it. Yeah, that was healthy. But it kept us warm. It was back to sleeping, and breathing fishing again. It is funny how things always seem to work out.

That summer and for many summers to come, Bob, who later was nicknamed Burdock, and I would go to the little lake that Pat and I fished for so many years, only now we were on the other side of the lake. We would use his gramps old wooden boat that was left in the brush. We would go fishing for perch. We fished the same place Dad and I did years earlier, by the red barn. My dad didn't fish much once he built his dream house, so it was Burdock and me, and sometimes Tiny. You guessed it, Tiny was his nickname. We called him Tiny because he was a big fourteen-year-old, two hundred pounds.

We fished every day after chores or after church. When haying time or threshing time came, farming took over. I learned to enjoy all of the things we did probably because I knew they were temporary and when they were done, we could go fishing. After a few years Gramps's boat began to leak. Burdock would fish and I would bail water from the bottom of the boat, and then we switched. It finally got so bad we almost sank one day. So we saved up our farming money—$1 an hour for baling hay or picking rocks—and we bought a $150 fourteen foot aluminum boat and left it at Gramps's place on the lake. We grew up farming, fishing, biking, and just plain having fun. I don't ever recall sitting down and watching TV. Burdock, Tiny and I were always doing something outside.

When we got old enough, fourteen or so, we started hunting pheasant on Gibby's land. That took over most of our fall fishing time. We didn't have a hunting dog, so we learned how to flush pheasant, so they would fly, without a dog and become quite proficient at shooting birds.

Burdock and I did find a dog at the local dump, and he followed us home.

Why would I find a dog at the local dump you ask? Back then there was a local dump, kind of like a landfill today. If you lived in the region, you could bring your garbage to the dump. Not only garbage, but anything you wanted to get rid of. Every Saturday Burdock and I would go to the dump to see if we could find anything valuable. And many times we did. We found money in old couches. We found old usable fishing poles. Then one day there was this old dog, a mutt. He followed us home and no one ever claimed him, so he became mine.

Mom let me keep him. He was my first dog and I named him Speedy. We'd always had dogs, but they were Dad's dog or Mom's dog. This was Dale's dog. He was a good dog, and we had plenty of fun with old Speedy. After a year or so he ran away, probably back to dump to follow another youngster home.

# CHAPTER 19

# LOVE AT FIRST SIGHT

Then it happened. I was Sixteen years old, I got my driver's license, bought a car, and now there were girls. Fishing went on the wayside for a while. There were park dances. There were parties. There were girls. I had been working on the farm making money and saving a little. When I turned sixteen, Mom told me that if I got my driver's license and wanted a car, I would have to have enough money to pay for the car and six months' of car insurance. I saved up until I had $500. I got my driver's license and bought my first car—a 1959 ford station wagon for $50.

And then I found out about girls. I also found out that girls were sure expensive. It seemed the ones I liked Burdock liked, but we never argued over a girl. It always seemed to work out.

Then my life changed. I would never be the same person again. I was sixteen and a half. My brother-in-law got me a job at the local supermarket as a stock and carry-out boy. I would stock shelves, and as a carry-out boy, I would carry groceries out to people's cars for them. This was not any supermarket, though. This one employed an eighteen-year-old deli manager, Sis, who would become my bride of forty-five years.

It didn't start out as love at first sight for me, although for her it was. I was going steady with a girl at the time, the one I knew I would marry. That lasted two months. I guess my first girlfriend didn't know she was going to marry me, or why would she have broken up with me?

Sis made me do all kinds of embarrassing things while I worked at the store. Like the time I was helping a customer with groceries when Sis was filling in as a check-out girl. My job was to bag all the groceries, put them in the shopping cart, and then bring the customer's groceries out to his or her car and put them in the trunk or backseat. This one customer had seven bags of groceries. After bagging them, I put them in a cart. As I was pushing the cart outside, I turned to look at Sis. She winked at me. I blushed and ran into the door and all groceries fell on the floor. All the glass items broke! It took me an hour to clean it all up. Do you know how hard it is clean up Miracle Whip and vegetable oil? So that was the beginning of a love affair that is still going on today.

After that love bit, for the next two years I was not thinking fishing thoughts morning, noon, and night. It was love, love, and more love. Every waking moment I wondered when would I see my love of my life again? Then, as fate would have it, I discovered that my future bride had grown up in a fishing family. Her father would fish every morning he wasn't working, which meant Saturdays and Sundays and four weeks of vacation a year. My bride-to-be had the fishing gods with her whenever she fished. The first time we went fishing together, she out fished me, catching two fish to my every one.

I didn't have much time for fishing, though. There were dances at night, car rides and school during the day, and in the summer I worked to pay for the dances and car rides. Even my buddies thought that was the end of my fishing days. Many warned me that the only reason Sis was going fishing with me was to keep me from other girls. What they did not know was she was truly a fisherwoman and was thrilled that she had found someone to fish with besides her dad and four brothers.

Eighteen years of age, high school graduation, now what am I going to do with my life? Fishing guide, bum, construction worker, mill worker like my father …? And so my life unfolded.

# CHAPTER 20

# TIME TO SORT LIFE OUT

After talking to one of my best friends, Hare—
how we became friends is again another whole
chapter in my life—I decided to work after
graduation instead of going on to school. But
before starting to work full-time, Hare and
I decided to go up to the Upper Peninsula
and stay at my father's friend's deer-hunting
camp and sort out what we were going to do
with our lives. As much as an eighteen- and
twenty-year-old could figure out. We packed a
few provisions—mostly beer—and, of course,
fishing poles. We stayed for a week and only
talked about the future for a short time. We

drank beer and fished in the stream for brook trout.

My cousin Ernie had taught me the fine art of stream fishing for brook trout. Small hook baited with a night crawler or the tale of chub, walk in the stream or brook and cast downstream into the holes. He must have taught me well as we would catch our limit of brook trout, every day (five each). We ate fish, drank beer, fished and talked and laughed and almost blew up the camp.

Almost blew up the camp?

They say every experience in life is really just a learning experience, and this experience was by far a learning experience. What *not* to do. We weren't at the camp but only a couple of hours when we went through the checklist that we'd gotten for how to "Open the Camp."

1. Unlock the door.
2. Open windows. (We didn't. Big mistake!)
3. Get firewood.
4. Make bed arrangements.

5.  Light the gas stove.

I asked my buddy if he'd ever lit a gas stove. He said no, but he'd seen someone do it once. How hard could it be? Turn on the LP tank outside—check. Open over door on stove—check. Light match—check. Put match in front of pilot light—check. There was no on/off pilot light; the gas was either on or off. After we'd tried four or five matches, the pilot light would not light. What else could we do? Have a beer and talk about what to do. Of course, the whole time gas is flowing into the oven. After a short time I tried to light the pilot light again. The next thing I know I'm on my back lying across the room. My buddy is laughing as he turns off the LP tank. Not only did I get blown across the room (no injuries) but all four windows in the camp were broken completely. That's why we were supposed to open the windows.... Well, we went to town and replaced the window panes and stayed for the week. And yes, we did get the stove lit, without any further explosions.

It was then back to the real world. All wasn't lost. My buddy and I decided we were going to join the military. It was 1968—Vietnam War. We knew a few friends who enlisted in the army, went to 'Nam, and didn't come back. No army for us, and surely not Marines for the same reason—infantry! We decided on the air force. Come fall we would take a test to see if we qualified and what the government thought would be the best area for us to work in. We actually believed the recruiter that *we* could pick the area of schooling we wanted and pick what part of the world we would be stationed. We did not want to join in June and miss our whole summer and all the fishing. And once we got to choose where we'd be stationed, of course we were thinking anyplace where there was water so we could fish on our days off. Eighteen-year-olds are sure naive.

Summer came and went. In October of that year we took the test for the air force. Not joined, just tested. My buddy qualified in the tech area, medical equipment repairs. To this day I do not recall what area of expertise the government had in mind for me. Hare did join the service and spent four years in medical equipment repair. To this day I do not know why he asked to be stationed in Minot, North Dakota, for four years. Oh, how naive …

CHAPTER 21

# CAUGHT UP IN LOVE

I never made it into any branch of service. Good or Bad? Not sure, but the good Lord had other plans for me.

I graduated from high school in June 1968 and Sis (Sis is my present day bride) was expecting our first child in February 1969. There were decisions to be made. Get married? Go into the air force? Get a mill job to support a family? My parents said I was too young to get married—even though my mom was eighteen when she got married!

You see, in 1968 in the state of Wisconsin you needed your parents' permission to marry if you were under twenty-one. (But I could join the military without my parent's say-so?) I went to our parish priest, but he said he would not marry us. He said we were too young and our chances of staying married were one in a million. Of course he was right but his boss must have not agreed. As of this writing we have been married for forty-five years and have three incredible children.

A mill job was a great option for earning a living and raising a family. There was Lots of money to be made. Besides, Sis's father worked in the mill, as did my father and many of my uncles. It was shift work; 7 a.m. to 3 p.m., or 3 p.m. to 11 p.m., or 11 p.m. to 7 a.m. That gave me a lot of time to fish. Now I was thinking clearly again.

Of course, I spent that winter of '68 finding an apartment and getting things ready for the baby and working. No one told me about overtime in the mill and working seven days a week. Also, according to union rules, if your relief person, the one did the same job as you but came in when your shift was done, didn't show, you had to stay and work another eight hours. I guess there is no fishing that day. My bride knew how miserable I was not being able to fish for weeks on end. She came up with a great plan.

## CHAPTER 22

# MY FIRST BOAT

Sis said to me, Maybe we should buy a small fishing boat for perch fishing? Was it possible? Could we afford it? Well, like any nineteen–year-old, I decided of course we could afford it. We'd make payments. We went looking for a boat and in June 1969 we found a great one—a new fourteen foot boat for $600 with a trailer. We also found a used 10HP motor for $125, a 1950 Mercury model that was only used to go to Canada for one week every year. It was in great shape and was exactly what we were looking for. (How we knew what we were looking for, I do not know.)

I turned down the overtime at work and fished every day I could. Sis was stuck at home with a baby while I fished. Even at age nineteen I knew that situation would not last. One day she announced "Let's get a babysitter and I'll go fishing with you." How could life get any better? My true love and myself would be fishing together, and she really did enjoy the fishing. The grandparents babysat and we fished, but that got real old in a hurry. The grandparents did not want to babysit as often as they used to. I guess the good Lord had a different plan for us. (Is this why I didn't drown when I was seven?)

They make life jackets for kids as young as one, so starting in the spring of 1970 our first child would go fishing with us every fishing outing. Mostly she played or slept in the boat, but she did catch some fish along the way. We fished every day we could. Sis still caught two fish to my every one, but who cared? I had married in 1968 and had a wonderful little girl and great supportive bride, and I could fish just about every day.

## CHAPTER 23

# THE BOBBER WENT UP AND DOWN AGAIN

Seventeen months after our daughter was born, we had a son. He would learn to fish from his father just as I had learned from my father. But wait. Our house rule was no child in the boat until they were six months old. Now what? My wife tells me to fish with my daughter and she would stay home with the newborn. I was too young or dumb to realize that I was babysitting and giving her a break. It all worked out.

My son was born July 14, 1970; on July 25, 1970, my dad was diagnosed with lung and brain cancer. Age fifty-five. By December he was gone. He never got a chance to fish with his grandson. My fishing mentor was gone. Why? I was mad at God for many years because he took Dad so early.

In November of 1970 I got laid off from my job. My first and only time out that I was unemployed. I was unemployed for 30 day. Every day while I was off I would walk the eight blocks to the lake to ice fish for perch. I walked because Sis needed our only car for errands. I would fish from morning to dark and walk back home and clean fish. We would fry fish, bake fish, can fish, eat more fish, and the next day do it all over again. At least we wouldn't starve. I thought it was good therapy, but while fishing I kept thinking of Dad being so sick and what could I do to help him. Not much.

I realized later in life that Dad taught me more than just fishing. I learned by example. He did what it took to provide for his family, and that's what I was doing. By fishing every day, morning to night, putting food on the table, I was using the lessons I learned when I was a little guy and did not even know it.

# CHAPTER 24

# THE TRADITION PASSES ON

As time went by my kids became fishermen too, not because they wanted to but because Dad wanted them to. At the young age of twenty-one, I thought I was a patient man, but I really didn't have a great amount of patience. (That would come way later in life). My obsession with catching fish took over the enjoyment of *fishing*. I would yell at the kids for missing a fish, for not hooking it properly, or not using a landing net. It was not very relaxing to take the kids fishing.

"Dad, put a worm on for me." "Dad, take the fish off." "Dad, I have to go to the bathroom."

"Dad, I'm tired." "Dad, he/she is fishing in my spot."

My saint of a spouse would always catch more fish then all of us. Her line was in the water more than mine and the kids' lines were tangled, and it was Dad's job was to untangle them. Of course, the kids would always say the same thing—I don't know how it happened!

But you know, two out of three of my kids became great fishermen through all the yelling and me forcing them to clean the fish. They actually enjoyed fishing, or is it more like a dog's attachment? Man's best friend likes to do whatever his master is doing, whether it's taking a walk lying next to you while you are reading, or watching you cut the lawn. The dog just enjoys being with you. And that was the case with the kids. And that was and is a good thing

So I thought at the time that they enjoyed fishing. Maybe, just maybe, we did something right when raising them and they enjoyed the company of their parents. *They* say that your children learn what they see and what they hear, and in our case it worked. From our fishing days they learned patience, camaraderie, respect, and that everything is a tradeoff.

CHAPTER 25

# THE SECRET

Back to, the secret of catching more fish. It only took me thirty years to learn this and I didn't learn it directly from my father. I learned it from my spouse. Yes, I said it. I learned the most valuable lesson in life, and not just fishing, from my wife.

It won't take a whole chapter but a simple sentence to expose everyone to this valuable lesson. Here we go.

You can catch more fish by having your line in the water than you can by not having your line in the water.

I know you're saying, Duh that's pretty obvious. Well, I have fished with literally thousands of people and I can't tell you how many times people fish with one bait and then change to another, and then another, and all that time their line is out of the water. And guess what? The person who left his line in the water caught the most fish. Surprise, surprise.

But what in the world does this have to do with lessons on life?

One: I have known people throughout my life, some may have lost their jobs or wanted to change careers. The ones that succeeded were the ones who spent as much time as possible looking and applying for jobs (line in the water). The people that seemed not to get the kind of jobs they wanted were always waiting for the phone call or hoping someone would tell them about a job or just plain talking about doing something different (line out of the water).

Two: Then there are people who say, I'm lucky, since things always seem to happen to me. I got the right job, the right spouse, good kids, sufficient money, and good health. These people, in reality, make all those things happen. They look for and pursue the right job, they work at their marriages through sacrifices, they spend time with their children, and they learn how to save. They do whatever it takes to become lucky (line in the water). Then there are the unlucky ones. "I never have good luck. This job sucks. I wish someone would offer me a better one. My spouse is unbearable to live with, It seems the only time we are happy is when we are apart. She always complains, so I don't even listen anymore. My kids are always in trouble. Why don't the teachers straighten them out? I never have any money; I wish my wife wouldn't spend so much." Someone else always causes their problems (line out of the water).

The lesson of life is truly about having your line in the water (LIW). You see, the more you do to help yourself, the better opportunities you will encounter. If you wait for things to happen, they never will. Life will pass you by. You will never really be happy. Life is all about enjoying every moment of time. A quote I have lived by for most of my life is as follows: The definition of success is doing what you want to do, becoming what you want to become, and being with whom you want to be with.

It is my belief that if you live with the line-in-the-water approach to life, you can become successful in your own way.

# Chapter 26

# My Second Passion in Life

After bouncing around from job to job and only staying at a job for six months to a year, I was trying to find out why I'd been put on this earth. Besides to fish, that is. After searching and searching—LIW—I found my calling in sales. My first sales job was not just in sales, but selling life insurance. Fortunately I didn't know at the time that it was the hardest sales job anyone could ever have—selling to people who needed your product but did not believe they needed it. (No one ever really thinks we are going to die or become disabled.) But let's back up a ways and talk about how I ended up in insurance sales.

Deep down I knew I wanted to be in sales. It just was one of those things. When I was twenty-three I was working for a business as a truck driver. I asked the owner of the company if I could apply for a job in sales. His response was, "You just don't have the talent to be in sales" (line out of water). I even offered to work for the same pay I was making driving a truck. I suggested that if I didn't succeed after six months, I would go back to truck driving (LIW). He told me before he could even consider my offer I needed to get some training in sales (line out of the water).

Shortly after starting my career in the insurance business, my mentor Harry H. Rhyner suggested I get involved in the Insurance Institute of Higher Education program. It involved taking an advanced business-planning course to better understand how to help business owners. I decided it was a great idea, so I took the one course. It did help me relate better to some business clients. I began working with many types of businessmen and became quite successful at helping them.

Over the next six months, I took another business course. Between working, helping raise three children, and fishing (of course), I was not able to spend as many hours studying per week. It took me three months to complete the course. After completing the course, my confidence level again increased substantially.

One day while on the water trolling for fish, I had lines in the water and for some reason the light went on. If I could catch more fish with more lines in the water, maybe if I took more courses in the insurance business, I could use the knowledge to help more people succeed at their goals. In the process I would make more sales and more money. It took me more than ten years of day and night school and correspondence courses to complete the entire course I had set out to do. I ended up with the equivalent of five years of college and two associate degrees, in business and insurance.

Would I have taken all those extra courses had it not been for LIW? Probably not.

Did the extra education directly put more money in the bank? Not necessarily, but it did provide me with a well-rounded education. I could now better communicate with different people from all walks of life. Thank God for LIW.

After some soul searching and guidance from some great line-in-the-water people, I enrolled in the Dale Carnegie Sales course at a cost of three quarters of a month's salary, which in 1973 amounted too $350. It was a fourteen-week sales course that altered my life. You see, they taught *line in the water* life lessons. At the time I took that course, I was working sixty hours a week driving a truck. The Dale Carnegie course was four hours a night once a week. I was also working part-time with no pay, training in insurance sales. Also I volunteered at a local boys club two hours a week, and of course I fished almost every weekend.

After completing the Dale Carnegie course, when I was twenty-four—a course, by the way, that did not really focus on sales but primarily on building self-confidence—I approached my employer again with the proposition to work in sales. Again he told me I just didn't have the talent. It was my good fortune that one of the salespeople working for the firm overheard my proposal to the owner. He told me that an old army friend of his was looking for good salespeople and set up a meeting with his friend for me.

As they say, the rest is history. I left the company I had been with for four years, with its job security, health insurance, and good pay, and went to work as an insurance sales agent for the largest insurance company in the world. I was surrounded by very successful insurance salesmen, and so my sales career started.

It wasn't all roses, though my first year was very successful. I won many awards. Back then that seemed important. I was asked to share my knowledge with people who were just starting out in the business. My first speech was about line in the Water, but I didn't know that was what I was talking about at the time. You see, my success came not from being a great salesman but from all lessons I learned from fishing.

My job as a new insurance salesman was to call people on the phone or talk to them eyeball to eyeball, so I did something very few sales people do. I listened to the manager, my mentor in sales. He said, "If you want to make money and be successful, the formula is very simple. Make one hundred phone calls a week; have three appointments a day scheduled, and of that talk eyeball to eyeball to two of them; and meet in person ten businesspeople a week." LIW. I did exactly as he stated, mostly because I did not know any better, and I was awarded top rookie of the year my first year. The rookie who was awarded second place made fifty calls a week, had seven appointments a week, and saw three or four people a week, and was always waiting for someone to call him (line out of the water).

Remember I said earlier that I'm not the smartest guy in the world, but I'm not afraid of hard work.

Did I mention that when I started in the insurance business, the year was 1974, one of the biggest recessions in our history at the time? Some places had 15 percent unemployment, interest rates on mortgages topped 12 percent. Thank God I did not know there was a recession. I just went out and did what I was told. LIW.

Life in sales wasn't always great. In the first five years in sales I quit a few times, for at least a day or a week. Every time I got motivated to get back to sales it was because I realized I was in the line-out-of-the-water mode not line in the water. It was incredible. When I did not see a lot of people, my sales and income went down. When I saw a lot of people—LIW—sales and income went up.

How is it possible that fishing would teach me the lessons I needed to be a successful person in life?

Shortly after I completed the Dale Carnegie course I started my long career in insurance and financial products. I had no formal training in sales but I knew that's what I wanted to do.

My mentor and the man that took a chance on me was Harry H. Rhyner. The bottom line, he said, was that I needed to make a lot of cold calls on the telephone, calling people I did not know, to be successful. He had eight other salespeople working for him at the time. I noticed that most of the salespeople called forty or fifty people per week and set up five or six meetings. They made one or two sales. After a short time, I figured it out. Line In The Water. (LIW). Just like fishing, the more lines in the water, the greater the chance of catching more fish.

If I made more calls, I would get more meetings and therefore make more sales. Just as Harry Rhyner suggested, I set a goal of one hundred calls a week over a four-day period. I always took off work on Fridays. One hundred calls netted twelve to fifteen appointments, which got me three to four sales. It worked just like fishing. I continued to use that approach for many years. Then one day while I was fishing in a great spot that always seemed to have fish around it, another light went on.

I was calling people I did not know, which was like fishing in an area that had few fish. Why not call people I knew, or someone I knew who knew someone else, like fishing where I knew there were fish?

The next day I started the approach of referrals, people who were referred to me by someone else. It worked from that day forward. I made fewer calls to people I didn't know and more to referrals. Kind of like following a fishing report that tells me when the fish are biting.

At the end of my career, 100 percent of my sales came from referrals. Thank God for LIW.

It truly allowed me to be successful. I was able to retire from the financial field at a young age and spend all of my time fishing, my true passion in life.

CHAPTER 27

# OH YEAH I'M MARRIED NOW

The kids were getting older and my spouse was getting restless staying at home raising them, but on weekends we fished. At this point I learned what my father had been trying to teach me so many years earlier while fishing—it's not about the catching of fish, it's all about the fishing. I didn't get upset when we fished all day and only caught three fish. It didn't matter if the fish were small. What mattered was that we were fishing (LIW).

Another area I became proficient at on the job was organization. I was one of the few highly organized salespeople in our industry. I could get more done in six hours than others could in twelve. Fishing made me organized! How, you ask, can fishing make you organized? Did you ever look in most fishermen's tackle boxes? Everything in its place!

Let's go back to the early days of fishing.

Once we finally had a boat, in order to take the kids fishing we needed to make sure we had packed all we needed, especially for camping trips to remote areas. Pack extra cloths, life jackets, fishing poles, bug spray, etc. The boat lights had to work, gas in the car, bait, food. The first trips were not very successful. We asked the kids to pack what they needed, only to arrive at our location with missing shoes or clothing. We soon learned that if we were going to have an enjoyable trip we needed to be organized, plan for the unexpected and bring things like rain gear. That's another story.

So as my career unfolded in insurance sales, so did my fishing lessons. On Sunday nights I would make out a list of things I needed to do the next day and the next week. Early Monday mornings I would put together all the things I needed for the day, as well as "rain gear" for the unexpected. I didn't have time to visit other salespeople to see how their weekends went or chat with the secretaries about their children. It was all work while at work (LIW). I knew where I was going on a sales call and knew what to bring. I didn't always know what to say, but that came with experience.

My mentor always told me that once I'd been on 5,000 eyeball-to-eyeball meetings with people, I would have heard just about all the objections to buying insurance that I would ever hear. I wanted to get to that 5,000 plateau as soon as possible. I looked at it like fishing, more time on the water, the better the chances of catching something. The more people I saw, the better chance I'd get proficient at sales. I did just that. Sold a lot of life insurance and gave hundreds of people peace of mind.

# Chapter 28

# Giving Back

After ten years of doing my own thing, I realized it was time to give back. Just as many people had taken the time to teach me fishing lessons and sales lessons, I needed to mentor others.

The opportunity of a sales manager position was offered to me and I excepted the position. My manager days were short lived. After three years in management, I realized that few people will follow the LIW approach. Most came into the industry as lines out of the water and never became line in the water. I did learn that large corporations sometimes work with the line-out-of-the-water approach. My employer and

I locked horns and parted ways. I went back to sales and was only responsible for myself.

Life became more exciting for our family during that thirteen-year period. Lots happened during that time frame some bad mostly good. As our children grew, we bought a new home and car and, of course, newer and bigger boats. Sis was now working outside the home. We had all of that and our health, but we sent many loved ones to the gates of St. Peter. My mother, brother, two grandmothers, my father and mother-in-law, a very close uncle (Uncle Lloyd) who taught me so much about courage. ( It would take Another book for that story.) There were some sad times, but we endured and learned to capture every moment in life.

There was a program in the insurance industry that asked experienced and successful salespeople to teach insurance-related courses to new salespeople at the generous rate of *free*. I was involved in the program for over ten years and mentored approximately three hundred students. Many of the students were LIW people and went on to become successful in their own right, not because of what I taught them as much as the direction we steered them. It seemed that no matter what the subject matter, it always came back to line in the water.

By this time I'd worn out a couple of boats and hadn't fished with many others besides my wife and kids, other family members, and a few friends.

CHAPTER 29

# NEW/OLD VENTURE

My cousin Ernie called from the Upper Peninsula to say that some guys were catching brown trout on the bay. Cousin Ernie was obsessed with fishing, although he preferred hunting to fishing. That was and is his passion. I learned with him that trout fishing was pretty much like all other fishing, with some added patience due to bug control on the trout streams. There always seemed to be a new batch of mosquitoes every time you went out. You only went trout fishing without bug spray once. I can attest to that! So began my long and ongoing journey of fishing, guiding, and chartering on the Great Lakes.

Ernie and I were about to go fishing for browns. I asked him what technique we would use to catch these browns. Ernie's response was, "How about we troll?" Trolling means you put a line in the water and drive the boat as slow as you can until you catch a fish. So Ernie's suggestion sounded good to me. The only lure we ever used other then live bait, was a Rapala. We only used a Rapala when fishing for Northern Pike. So we both decided that The Rapala would be our choice of lures for Brown Trout. What I didn't realize was how Ernie had already learned the "Line In The Water" approach to catching more fish. "Put a line in the water and troll for eight hours," he said, "and we are bound to catch something."

The Rapala was by far a great choice of baits We did catch a lot of fish.( When fishing for browns today 2013 we still use the same type of lure "The Rapala" Actually we fished just about every weekend and we were known by most of the locals as the boat to follow.

The Wisconsin Department of Natural Resources was responsible for the introduction and stocking of the brown trout. As the number of stockings increased, so did our daily catch limits, ranging from three to twelve pounds.

Soon word was out about the two guys in that white boat catching limits of brown trout. Family members and friends asked to go fishing for browns. I took them out and afterward they would give me money for gas. Pretty soon I wasn't reeling in any fish. The people I took out were reeling in all the fish and I was responsible for setting lines, driving the boat, and locating fish.

It was an awakening. I enjoyed watching people reel in a fish and then getting the fish in the landing net for them. So began my life as a guide and charter captain.

Ernie, on the other hand, took a few people out, but I think he liked fishing alone more than having people around.

I acquired my guide license and began getting paid to fish. How could life get any better? Sell all week and guide on Saturday. Sunday was family day. I was able to make enough money guiding to pay for all my personal fishing trips, the ones with the kids and my spouse.

It was amazing. More guiding trips generated more guiding trips, taking more people out, and more people would call for my service. More sales calls, more sales. Yes, line in the water was at work again. How can it be possible that something you hear over and over again when you're seven can truly set the standards for your life?

CHAPTER 30

# PATIENCE

On many guiding trips, which were generally six plus hours, sometimes we would troll for four hours without a fish or even a bite, Customers would say, "Let's give up and try again another time." The first couple of trips I agreed, but then the light went on." Line in the water." I started telling people, "Let's give it a little longer." Nine times out of ten, we would catch fish in the last two hours of the trip. Patience is really like" Line in the water", that is the more patients you have while fishing the longer you continue to fish and there for increase your chances of catching fish. It was a lesson I had learned so many years earlier from my father, Patients.

An example would be when you take the kids at an early age on a fishing outing. The fish are not biting and the kids are getting bored, they ask when are we leaving, they start to fight amongst themselves as all kids seem to do. You really have to have patients in that type of situation or the fun outing of the day could turn into very frustrating day.

I think the patients I developed when taking the kids fishing helped me succeed not only at fishing but also in everyday life situation and help me become a better person. You see, when guiding for fishing you have such a variety of people on board your boat. We had People from all walks of life, people with such different personalities that in itself can be very challenging. Patients, is required to cope with dealing with such a variety of people. You have to learn how to communicate with each and ever person. You must learn how to read or understand all the customers. Sometimes that was not an easy task.

By having patients and learning to communicate better while guiding a fishing trip, it taught me that patients will actually help you in everyday life situations. As an example, by waiting for a child to make a decision on some major event in their lives. Or when you are in sales and you are waiting for a customer to make a decision on buying or not buying your product.

It appears to me that the patients I showed from fishing, was passed on to my children and others. All three of my children seem to have more patients with their children then I did when I was their age. And differently all of the first mates that I have trained throughout the years learned the value of patients. They all seem to have a better understanding of the wait and see how things turn out.

In the end patients is ever so important. May it be fishing or just coping with what life offers. Without patients life can be ever so stressful.

# CHAPTER 31

# WAKE-UP CALL

Life was good, all was well, and line in the water was applying to most life situations, when *wham!*

Our youngest daughter, Kerry Jo, at age seven kept falling off her bike. The teacher said she couldn't see the board, so she moved her to the front of the class. Maybe she should go to an eye doctor. The eye doctor said, "I see something on our test that doesn't look right." What the hell did that mean? She said maybe we should go see a neurologist. A neurologist deals with the brain, not the eyes. Final result: "Your daughter has a brain tumor."

Life stops. How the hell can line in the water apply? Who cares! All we want is for our baby to be okay. Forget fishing, forget work. All we do is spend all our time in the hospital with our baby and pray. We pray and pray some more. Will she be okay? Will we lose her? How can her time be up?

After further tests by a specialist in a children's hospital we are told that she has a sodo tumor. That is a tumor that doesn't exist but does all the damage of a brain tumor unless it is treated. Options: a shunt, (a tube is inserted into the skull and a tube drains the fluid to the stomach) or just medications. We elect the medications. After six months the tumor is gone. All seems well.

Several years later we found that the medications had side effects—advanced body maturity. At twelve our daughter's body was more like a fifteen-year-old. But other than that, life was good. She grew up, married, and has three children.

I look back at that time and realize Dad's lessons did apply. After we were first told she had a tumor, my wife and I asked for a second opinion. And then we seen a third with a specialist. We called the doctors, set up the appointments, and finally found the one who specialized in sodo tumors. We took action, played offense, not defense, and it worked. Yes, line in the water did apply. If we had been in line-out-of-the-water thinking, who knows what would have happened. So yes, fishing lessons can help us get through many crises, and in some cases can save lives.

CHAPTER 32

# KIDS LEAVE—LINE
# IN THE WATER

Fishing continued, as did the challenges of life. By this time in my life my two older children were in high school. I was able to take off work for weeks at a time and was guiding for fishing on the largest lake in Wisconsin, Lake Winnebago, better known as" Bago." I was on the water every day for thirty days in June. People came to fish for lots of reasons:

1. Catch walleye
2. Catch freshwater fish
3. Learn how to fish for walleye (techniques)

4. Learn where to find fish

5. Or just wanted to say they fished on "Bago".

Word got out that I was the only guide on the north-northwest shore. Two local newspapers decided to do an article on my approach to bag trolling, mostly because I had applied many of the techniques from Lake Michigan fishing to walleye fishing, specifically using planner boards.

A planner board was a rectangular piece of hardwood with a 30° cut on the front and a six ounce weight on the bottom of the board. A metal eye hook was attached to the board, along with 150 feet of line. The line was also attached to the boat. We would then use spring-like clothes pins let out a certain amount of line. The clip would slide down the line some distance from the end of the board. The bottom line is, we could fish with six lines at once. That certainly increased our chances of catching more fish, but more importantly we covered more water to find fish. LIW.

The local newspapers each sent a reporter out on my boat to view this "new" technique. (I actually had been using it for twelve years.) The day was good. There were clear skies, calm waters, and many, four- to six-pound walleyes. That was a Saturday. On Sunday morning a picture and article were on the front page of both sports section (must have been a slow news day). The phone never stopped ringing for a week. Everyone wanted to learn how to use the boards. Line in the water still worked! I had perfected the perfect way to catch more walleye on "Bago". How could life be so simple?

Both of my older children were fishermen and they helped me immensely on my guiding trips. On these trips I would share with them ideas on having a plan in life, life on the water, and goals. But most importantly, how we should enjoy life.

## CHAPTER 33

# KIDS TEACH US A LESSON

My wife and I had goals for the two older children, who were seventeen months apart. Our oldest one, our daughter, was a gifted singer, an A/B student, very outgoing and very moody, and a good fisherman, although she did not spend all of her free time fishing with me as my son did. Our son was way too much like his father: a C/D student who liked sports and anything to do with the outdoors. I don't think there was a time that I fished when my son was not in school that he did not fish with me. He hunted, ice fished, went snowmobiling, etc. Chip off the old man's block. Our goal was to have Kelly, our older daughter, go on to college and become a performer or music teacher. We assumed that's what she wanted. For our son, our goal was to help him graduate, get a job in the local paper mill, and enjoy the outdoors. But just about the time you think you have it all figured out, life throws you a curve. Remember I said these were our goals. Apparently they were not theirs.

When Kelly, our oldest daughter, was a junior in high school, I asked her over dinner one night how she'd scored on the ACT test.

"I never took the test," she said. "That's for those kids that are going on to college."

You could have knocked me over with a pillow! "What do you mean you're not going to college? What do you plan on doing after high school?"

"I don't know but I'm not going to college, that's for sure."

I asked myself how the hell could I read a lake and tell you if the fish are biting but I did not know what my kid was thinking of at that moment? How did LIW apply here?

"But you love singing and the music teacher says you have a one in a million voice. You get great grades. So why not go to college?"

"Just because, that's why! She proclaimed"

Welcome to the world of a teenager.

After one full year of convincing, she agreed to go to the local college and major in performing. She worked several jobs since I informed her she had to pay her own way. She seemed to fit right in with college life and made lots of friends. She belonged to a few select music groups, including the show/jazz choir, which consisted of eighteen singers and dancers that went around the state performing. Man, I thought, we were right about her going to college.

During the summer between her sophomore and junior years, I came home from a fishing trip to find Kelly at the kitchen table and not in a very good mood. I asked what was wrong.

"I got this bill for next semester at the university and I don't want to go back to school."

I told her she was twenty-one years old and needed to make her own decisions in life. I was thinking a little reverse psychology would work here.

"Why are you going back to school if you don't want to?"

"Because you want me to," she said.

I told her that was a dumb reason. If she didn't want to go to school, then she shouldn't.

"Okay, I'm not going back."

What the hell just happened? That reverse psychology didn't work so well! When the fish aren't biting I change colors, but what do I do to convince her to continue her education?

After several days of pondering I decide she is twenty-one. She must make up her own mind. So much, for *our* goals. We needed to ask her about *her* goals.

It took a while but she finally found a career she enjoyed. She applied for a mill job in manufacturing. There were four thousand applicants for fifty positions. She got the job. She worked shift work, made a lot of money, and loved what she was doing. She was happy, not as moody. Her mill job lasted ten years and then she found it was time to move on. At present she is enjoying a career as a credit manager for a local company, she is married, and has a wonderful little boy.

Who would have guessed it? I learned a valuable lesson about kids and people. Like fishing, it's hard to predict what will happen that day. Our goal may be to catch ten fish but we only succeed in catching one. Life is always full of surprises. Well, looks like we'll have two children working in the mill....

My boy Dale Jr. (Bunky—his nickname)—came home from school in the middle of his junior year and told us he'd just enrolled at the local technical college.

"What?" I asked. I was thinking he'd quit high school and enrolled to get his GED.

"Bunky, don't you think it would be a good idea to finish high school instead of quitting?"

He looked at me and said, "Dad, what in the world are you talking about? I enrolled in the police science course at the technical college. I'm going to be a cop!"

How I kept my composure, I do not know. I asked him, "You do know you need better than a C average to go to college and it costs money? How do you plan on accomplishing all this?"

"Well, Dad, just like when you plan a fishing trip, I too have a plan. One, I will get my grades up. Two, I started a new job today as a cook at a local restaurant and will make enough this summer to pay for two years of college."

All this from a boy who, up until then, had never had a grade higher than a C, except for in gym. The boy whose sixth grade teacher convinced him and us that he would never be better than a C student. Boy, could I write another book on the whole education system.

Two years later Bunky had graduated from high school with a 3.6 GPA and had saved enough money to pay for one year of college. It seems he did have a plan. LIW. His girlfriend of two years was the valedictorian of their class. Seems like when my son said he was going to his girlfriend's house to study, they actually did study. She taught him great study habits. As far as work, he worked every weekend and many nights cooking and saving money. He graduated from college with an associate's degree in police science and a 3.5 GPA. We were and are so proud. But you know what?

He elected to take an offer from a company he had worked at part-time as a salesman and stayed there for four years. Never did become a cop. He spent another ten years at a different firm, eventually becoming the vice president of sales in the landscaping field. He was in charge of a three-state area. After ten years in the corporate world, he'd had enough. He took the plunge and became self-employed—I guess he did learn a few things from me—manufacturing and selling concrete countertops. He and his wife bought a little piece of land with an old barn. They remodeled the barn, which was over one hundred years old, and set up his business. He has been very successful in his endeavor and has been able to provide for his family of six children. The most important thing, he enjoyed every minute of all the careers he chose. LIW. He had a plan and it wasn't our goal, it was his.

Getting our two older children to leave the nest and become healthy, happy adults was very much like a fishing trip: plan, anticipate, get to your destination, and get back home. But really, it was all about the journey.

## Chapter 34

# Obsession Gets Worse

My fishing obsession got worse. I wanted to fish all the time. Every minute of every day I wanted to fish. I needed a plan, a great plan. How could I make a living with the same money and fish? Fortunately, I had a secretary who put me to work. We met with many people, helped them succeed at their goals, not mine. I'm convinced to this day that putting the customer first and doing what is right for them, not me, helped me become successful. Instead of spending the money I earned on new cars or expensive toys, I saved it. It didn't take long before I was able to work out a schedule of working only four days a week from April to September. As time went on I was able to reduce my schedule to three days a week, then two days a week, then one day a week. (Thanks to my secretary and friend Jennie, who handled all of the things that needed to be done at the office when I was not present at the office.)

Of course, you guessed it. I fished almost all the days I didn't work. Paying customers paid me to fish. How could life be so good? I had charter fishing trips four or five days a week. We got a bigger boat to accommodate more passengers. What a great life for me.

How about my marriage? With me fishing all the time, my wife decided she didn't want to fish as much as she had in the past. (She tells everyone that I hollered too much at her. Well, maybe I did way back then.) Thank God the good Lord blessed me with a woman who allowed me to enjoy my passion. She really did not and still does not mind me fishing all the time. I think it goes back to her childhood. Her father was an alcoholic and her parents fought all the time. Her dad was in the tavern when he wasn't working, and when he was home they fought constantly. None of that occurred in our marriage, and I think she truly enjoys the fact that our marriage is so different from her parents'.

Even though I fished all the time, I was not a drinker. Matter of fact, I don't touch any alcohol at all, not for the last twenty years. I'm not sure if it was the nondrinking or that we were truly made for each other, but we never argued about anything. So I would fish and she would do her thing, whether it was bowling, knitting, making cards, socializing, or spoiling the kids. When someone asks how long we've been married, my brides response would be, we have now been married for forty-five years but only together for twenty-two years. You see, the whole time we've been married Dale has not been home half the time because he's been fishing. I cannot argue.

CHAPTER 35

# PROUDEST ACCOMPLISHMENT

It may seem like I fished morning, noon, and night, but that is not true. If I fished one hour or eight hours a day I was happy, just as long as I fished every day that I could. Actually, of all things I've accomplished in my short lifetime, the greatest accomplishment is this. I attended 100 percent of all three of my children's school activities, from kindergarten all the way through their high school years, from parent/ teacher conference to sports and music activities. (LIW.) And to this day all three children still tell others that I attended so many activities. It was not easy, but I made up my mind early in our marriage that I would accomplish this goal. I'm guessing it's because my father and mother only attended one of my activities throughout my school years. Right or wrong, I always felt bad that they did not see me perform in sports or whatever activity I was in.

Life continued on pretty uneventfully for many years, and then came along grandkids. As Sis says, "If I'd known how much fun grandkids would be, I would have had them first!" So blessed are we to have ten grandkids. With encouragement and our line-in-the-water teaching to our kids, one of our children, Bunky and spouse Sharon, became a foster parents to needy children and took in three children two were sisters age 5 and age 7 up until this point the girls had been in 5 foster homes, the 3rd a little boy 7 months old who was taken away from his mother by the state for she was unable to care for him due to a mental issue. Bunky and his family, adopted all three of the children. This is also the family whose one son Brady, was born without a left arm. That could be another book in itself, for he is now eighteen and has taught us all the true meaning of never giving up.

Life has become very hectic again, as now we are watching our grandkids grow, and of course for me, this is new blood to teach or curse with fishing. Turns out that of all the grandkids, only two truly enjoy fishing. Because I learned this from my children, I let the grandkids do what they want to do not what we want them to do. Of course, I do realize that it might not be the fishing the grandkids like, but that being with Grandpa is the true enjoyment.

## CHAPTER 36

# THE YOUNGEST

They say the youngest is always the favorite and gets away with more than all the other kids. In our case, *they* are right. Kerry Jo did not like to fish. As a matter of fact, she didn't even eat fish. She by far gave us the most grief as a teenager. All the things I learned from the older ones never seemed to apply to her. As my charter fishing continued to be my focus, I tried to help her succeed at what she wanted. Since 1976, my wife and I had taken a ten-day trip every year to some great location in the United States. No kids. It was like a honeymoon every year. Now it was time to bring our baby along. You would think I would have learned from the first two to ask what she wanted, but I assumed she wanted to go on vacation with us. Of course she did not. That was one of the longest trips we had ever been on. Our daughter was mad for ten days.

One thing led to another with our little Kerry Jo. She started skipping school, hanging out with the wrong kids, and just plain being a teenager. A frequent phone call began, "Mr. Laurin, could you come to school to discuss your daughter's situation again?" Somehow she graduated from high school, and then she announced, "Dad, I'm going to attend school for cosmetology in the fall!"

This came from a child who almost quit school.

"And how are you going to pay for school?" I asked.

"Well, I have a plan. I've been working at one job and I'll get two more jobs and save my money and maybe you can help me out and I'll pay your back."

A plan, like planning a fishing trip, but she never liked fishing. Again I realize what fishing is. It's not the fishing. It's really what life is all about, and she learned that.

She did go to school and graduate. She did pay for her school and paid me back. She did get married and has three children and now loves to eat fish, although she still doesn't like to catch fish. Like her brother she had a plan—LIW—and she is truly an entrepreneur. She has worked at waitressing, Mary Kay sales, sales office work, cleaned houses, made and sold purses, and many more jobs. I tell her that her business card should be the size of a billboard to have room for all her careers. She tells me she just needs to find her passion. Recently she finally found her passion—a certified yoga instructor. She eats, sleeps, and breathes yoga, and now is finding it important to build a clientele. (LIW)

Wow. How can fishing help other people?

## CHAPTER 37

# TIME TO FISH FULL-TIME

At fifty-seven I retired from my financial planning practice and now charter fish from mid-April to mid-September every year. We bought another bigger boat and moved it to a new marina. There about ten other charter fishing boats at the marina. For some reason many of the captains thought I was stealing customers from them. I always kept to myself and just catered to my customers' needs. After several seasons I realized most captains were more concerned about how many fish they caught and, more importantly, if they caught more than the other captains. My thoughts on charter fishing were and are: it is the experience of being on Lake Michigan and on a fishing boat, not how many fish you catch. We make sure our customers have a great time, and the catching is secondary.

As I was the new kid on the block at this marina, I just went along and did my own thing. For example, most captains would leave port at 4 a.m. I left, and still leave, at 5:30 for my morning charter fishing. I promote afternoon charters that run from 1:30-7p.m. I have found some people want to experience fishing on Lake Michigan but have no desire to get up at 3 a.m. to do so. Kind of like asking the kids what their goals are, not mine. The fact is, we are very successful at catching fish in the middle of the day, and many other charter boats have caught on to afternoon fishing.

LIW applies to fishing, but really fishing is just a way to help all of us who are obsessed with fishing cope with everyday life. So the next time you or someone you know says "wet a line" (go fishing), enjoy what Mother Nature has to offer. Stop and think how fishing and life really do parallel each other. LIW may sound like a fishing term, but it tells us how to live our lives to the fullest.

## CHAPTER 38

# TEACHING A FIRST MATE AGAIN

After years of either operating my boat alone or have someone else drive my boat for me, I finally got my first," First Mate". I must have had sixteen or eighteen first mates through out the years. Some stayed for a year or two, others a couple of weeks. Some were good, some were average, and some were not so good. I have a niece whose son Alex loved to fish. I mean, obsessed with fishing.

When he was fourteen he had the maturity of a twenty-year-old, and he became my full-time mate all summer, from June through

August. He was a natural and caught on after two days of training.

He worked for me for four summers, and I continued to teach him. I even helped teach him how to drive a truck so he could get his driver's license. Apparently he listened well to all of my teaching. He learned at a young age to pick his friends wisely and was able to stay on the straight and narrow all through his high school years.

I have way too many stories about Alex, whom I nicknamed Smiley because of his contagious smile. Seasons came and seasons went, and Smiley made very good money. After his high school graduation, he lived on board the *Fishhook*, my boat, until October of that year. When we pulled the boat out of the water for the season, he was forced to find an apartment. Fishing was fun with Smiley and customers loved him.

One day I realized that the student, Smiley, had succeeded at his learning. When we would come into port with a large catch of the day, many people would come over to see how we had done. They'd ask Smiley, "What worked today to catch so many fish?" He would answer and move on. No one asked me, the captain with forty years of experience, and I was okay with that.

One evening I overheard Smiley tell one of his friends, "Dale drives the boat, but I catch all the fish. I don't know how he'll catch fish when I'm not here."

One would think I'd be upset, but it was one of the greatest compliments I could have gotten. The student was moving on to being a teacher. He had learned well.

CHAPTER 39

# AN INSPIRATION

As I mentioned before, my grandson Brady was born without a left forearm. He's a feisty kid. His parents divorced when he was two, and they have had joint custody. Brady's passion is sports—talking sports and playing sports. In high school he played varsity baseball, football, and basketball. Did I mention he has no left forearm or hand?

Brady is my new student and First Mate. Several years ago I asked him if he wanted the job as a First Mate. He said yes. I tried him out for a week. He passed!!!! He was able to perform 90 percent of the tasks. Brady just needed more training on a few things and to brush up on his people skills.

Now you have to understand IN SPORTS, Brady didn't just make the team and sit on the bench. He participated as a player. He was recently named defensive player of the year by his basketball coach. What does this have to do with fishing? Well, Brady has had to work one hundred times harder than you or I to get to where he is in sports and in life. Maybe I admire him so much because of how hard I had to work at things in life. Just like Brady. He has practiced LIW since the time he was three. He didn't know it at the time, but his LIW was hours and hours of throwing a baseball, a basketball, and a football. It paid off.

I have watched him grow into a confident young man. When times are tough and something doesn't go right for me, I stop and say to myself, "If Brady can do this and he only has one arm, I certainly can make it work with two."

One never knows who the real teacher is in life….

## CHAPTER 40

# ANOTHER THING IN LIFE: THE MARATHON

You would think by age forty-eight, one would have learned a lot about LIW, but I guess not. Remember, I'm a slow learner. It was 1998. Two of my four sisters decided to walk the local marathon, 26.2 miles. During their training they asked me to join them for the race. I elected to participate in the race and train with them, even though I was overweight and out of shape. The training would cut into my fishing time. So my training involved riding my bike ten to fifteen miles a day for one and a half months leading up to the race. My sisters walked, lifted weights, and ate right (LIW).

Marathon day and we all start out with lots of energy. My goal is thirteen miles, not the whole 26.2. After thirteen miles I'm feeling great, so I continue. At mile marker twenty I hit *the wall*. My sisters continue on and I go to the first aid station. Twenty minutes later I get my second wind and finish the race. I finished 745 out of 745 finishers, in seven hours and forty-five minutes. I had to be carried to my car. I could not get out of bed for twenty-four hours. It took me a couple of weeks to recover.

I completed the marathon and learned a valuable lesson about life. LIW applies again.

Six years later my grandson, daughter, and son-in-law and myself, decided to walk/run the marathon. Again, I'm a slow learner, but this time I trained, gave up some fishing so I could walk, run, bike, stretch, and lift weights (LIW). We all finish the race in six hours twenty minutes, more than one and a half hours faster than my first race. I walked to my car after the race and got up early the next day to go to the gym. I walked four miles on the treadmill pain free. Instead of one line in the water, I had five or six in—in regards to my different types of training—and again fishing proved to help me be successful in other endeavors.

CHAPTER **41**

# THE POLAR PLUNGE

Like so many things I've experienced in life, the polar plunge was again a challenge.

The polar plunge is as follows.

It takes place in cold climate states like Wisconsin on January 1 at noon each and every year. Where I live, the air temp will average about 20°F and the water temp 32°-34° F. In our small town they cut a hole in the ice at a local boat landing, since by January the lakes are frozen over with ice up to fourteen inches thick. Approximately one hundred and fifty not entirely sane people meet on the shore thirty minutes prior to the plunge. At the sound of a starting gun, everyone runs into the ice-cold water. Some have tuxes on and others just swimsuits. Some girls even wear two-piece bikinis! I choose trunks and a T-shirt.

Once your body hits the water, panic sets in. You cannot help but hyperventilate, no matter how prepared you are. Some participants swim around for up to ten minutes in that 34° water! Others like me run in and then run out just as fast. Friends surround you with a blanket, and you discard your wet clothes and put on heavy winter apparel. Some go to the local pub to celebrate. I choose a cup of hot chocolate. From there I go home and take a hot twenty-minute shower. It seems to take the rest of the day to warm up!

Now doesn't that sound like fun? Remember, I said I wasn't the most intelligent person in the world. But like many other events I've been involved in my whole life, this one taught me a valuable lesson. When people ask me why in

God's name I would do the polar plunge, this is my answer.

"If I can survive the polar plunge on January first, there is nothing the good Lord can throw at me over the next 365 days that could be worse." And that is "not a word of a lie" this phrase was used by a good friend of mine (Bobby Mann).

## CHAPTER 42

# MORE LESSONS

Many years back, when charter fishing, I somehow got caught up in the competitive aspect of other charters. In other words, we wanted to know who had caught the most fish any given day.

I was very consistent year after year with the number of fish I caught. My average was six to eight fish per trip. I was right in the middle of the pack. Some boats had ten to twelve, had some two to four. But there was always that one boat. He always averaged about fifteen fish. You could fish next to him all day and have the same results. He'd have twice as many fish as you.

After I realized it wasn't the number of fish we caught that made customers happy, but the experience of fishing on the big water, I became content catching what we average still today: it is eight to ten fish per trip.

One sunny August day, after a morning trip and while I was preparing for the next day, the great Captain Joe, the one who averaged fifteen fish, stopped by to chat. After some usual captain talk, I asked him outright, "How come you always catch more fish than everyone else?"

He couldn't stop laughing. I asked what was so funny. He said, "Everyone thinks I have special tactics to catch more fish but I don't."

He asked me how many lines I fished with when I was on a charter. I said ten to twelve. He asked what my average catch per day was. I told him eight to ten.

"So here's my big secret," he said. "I run eighteen to twenty-one lines, two times as many as you. Do the math."

Wow! LIW. As the young people say, "Duh." Guess he knew all along about LIW. I thought I knew all about LIW but did not carry it out further. (Did I mention I'm not the most intelligent guy …?)

Later that season, my first mate said he was going to run nineteen lines. Needless to say we caught more fish. Did we stay at nineteen lines? No. Too many tangles, messes, and way too much stress. But the fact is, LIW applies again.

CHAPTER **43**

# FIRST-TIME FISHING
# EXPERIENCES

It still amazes me after chartering and guiding for forty years that everyone that who has fished on the Great Lakes remembers in great detail their very first trip. It might have been fifty years ago or just one year ago.

If someone you know has fished on the Great Lakes ask them, "Do you remember your first trip on Lake Michigan?" You might be surprised at the answer. It seems everyone enjoys a different experience on any fishing trip. Two people can be on the same boat the same day and remember two opposite experiences. Here are some of the stories told to me:

## 1

"I'm forty-two years old," Joe said, "and I remember it like it was yesterday. I was eight and my father had two boats. There were for charter fishing. So when he wasn't charting he would just go 'fun fishing.' I was old enough to go out on the big boat. I could hardly sleep the night before. We were up early at 3 a.m. to get to the boat. Out we went, and I could not wait to catch one of those big fish Dad had taken so many pictures of. We were not out more than thirty minutes when I said to Dad, 'I don't feel so good.' And just that fast, I threw up all over the back of the boat. Dad laughed. We stayed out for four hours. I was sick the whole time. I have no recollection of any fish, just that when we got back to port, Dad made me clean up the back of the boat!"

## 2

"I love to fish. I like to do a lot of things. I really like NASCAR." That is what Paul told me. Paul has been on my boat with his parents many times. Paul is nineteen but thinks like a twelve-year-old. He gets very excited about everything he does, so excited that he gets everyone else excited about whatever he's doing. He is one of those people you just enjoy being with.

This trip was his first. We were only fishing for about ten minutes when my first mate hollered, "Fish on." Paul's dad handed the pole to Paul. He reeled in a nice twelve-pound brown. It was the biggest brown of the season so far for our boat. He was so excited. His father had to take dozens of pictures before the day was over with. Paul caught three fish that day.

I have a pretty big boat, thirty-eight feet, and Paul was intrigued by all the equipment and accessories all over the boat. He had many questions. When it was time to go in, a thirty-minute ride back to port, I asked Paul if he wanted to drive the boat. Before I could finish my sentence, he was behind the wheel.

"Dad, take my picture."

So again, a dozen photos were taken. Paul was like a kid in a candy store, his smile from ear to ear.

Once I docked the boat with the help of some local marina people, one of the dock helpers looked at Paul and asked, "Did you catch any fish today, young feller?"

"Yeah," Paul answered, "but I drove the boat!"

Two weeks later his dad called to tell me that Paul put some pictures on his wall at home, what Paul calls his wall of shame, from our fishing trip.

I asked "was it the fifteen-pound salmon or the twelve-pound brown?"

His dad said, "No. He put up a picture of him driving the boat!!!"

## 3

"My first trip on the lake was out of Algoma, Wisconsin. I will never forget it," said Jim. "It occurred thirty years ago. Some guys at work got a deal with a charter boat, and we would be able to go out for about 50 percent off the price. I should have known better. We arrived at the dock and could not believe our eyes. The boat was old. I mean old and not so nice looking. The three of us looked at each other and hoped for the best. Once we left port the captain said, 'Hang on, I'm going to go full speed.' His definition of full speed and mine was as far apart as New York and California. Okay, we should be fishing in about an hour. An hour was six miles from shore. Halfway out to our destination, I saw a monarch butterfly. It passed us. That was the slowest boat I've ever been on. We did catch two fish each that day, but the boat is what I remember most."

## 4

Mary said, "My first and last trip was ten years ago. I did not like water and still don't. My husband said, 'I think you would love fishing on Lake Michigan.' I should have known better. We left port and the water was calm, so the captain said there were two to four foot waves. To me they looked like ten footers! I was scared to death. I never got off the chair. Finally we were fishing. I guess we caught some fish, but I don't remember how many. After about three hours I asked how long we were staying. My husband told me, 'Only for another two hours. Don't you wish we could stay all day?' I endured, but the icing on the cake came when I asked the captain how deep the water we were fishing in was. He said 200'. I couldn't even speak. I had been scared before. Now I was petrified.

We got back in safe and sound. The boys were happy with their catch, and I was happy to be on shore. I never went back."

## 5

It was a lot of years ago, Don said, when he had been on his first trip on the big pond. Don is eighty-six.

"I had bought a sixteen foot boat and took the two boys out for some lake trout fishing. My wife didn't approve, but I still went. The boys had never caught anything bigger than a ten inch fish before this trip. I really didn't know what I was doing as far as how to and where to fish. I talked to some guys at work that had done some of this type of fishing, so I brought what I needed and just went out. We caught four fish that day. The boys reeled in all the fish. I ran the boat. For years to come, the boys still talked about the first trip."

# 6

"It was 1985. I had been given a gift certificate for a fishing charter trip for two on Lake Michigan. Even though I lived only forty-five minutes from the lake, I had never been fishing on it. I'm a physician and never took the time to do a lot of outdoor things. But my receptionist booked a day for the trip and also asked my son, also a physician, to go along. We left late afternoon the day before the trip and stayed at a motel. That evening we went for dinner. We both realized that evening that over the last ten years, we had not taken much time to be together and just talk. We talked till early morning hours about family, kids, etc., but not work. I recall we didn't get much sleep that night. You know, I think we caught some fish that day, but I can't tell you how many or how big. I just remember spending time with my son."

## 7

"I'm twenty-one now. I was seven when my dad took me on a fishing trip with a guide for brown trout on Lake Michigan. I was so excited. I had caught northern pike through the ice but never a brown trout. We had to get up really early and drive. It seemed like hours, but I'm sure it wasn't more than one hour. The boat we were in was small. The guide put out six poles and said" watch the poles". It seemed again like hours before we had a fish on the line. I reeled in a seven-pound walleye, a ten-pound brown trout, and a six-pound smallmouth bass. The guide asked my dad if he was going to mount any of the fish for me. He said a picture would do.

"We took the fish home and all the way home I asked Dad if we could mount the big fish, but we just cut them up and ate them."

# CHAPTER 44

# STORIES OF FISHING CHARTER TRIPS

## WHERE THERE IS A WILL
## THERE IS A WAY

My uncle Lloyd, Cousin Ernie's dad, had rheumatoid arthritis and was in a wheelchair most of his adult life. He told me during a visit that he wished he could fish out of boat. Cousin Ernie and I lined up a trip to take him out for brown trout. We got a life vest on him, carried him to the boat, and fished. I don't remember if we caught fish or not, but I will never forget the feeling I had that day of helping such a great human being. By the way, Uncle Lloyd knew *line in the water* long before I did. He lived with his disease for twenty-five years and did not let it stop him from living.

## THE SMILE SAYS IT ALL

The trip was for two people, a father and his thirteen-year-old son. Father doesn't fish much, if at all. Son wants to fish all the time. We were fishing for brown trout, trolling. The son caught a twelve pound brown and was smiling from ear to ear. I asked him what was the biggest fish he ever caught up until now was a two pound bullhead, he told us. I don't remember if we got any more fish that day, but for the whole six hours that smile never left the boys face. I truly believe from that day forward he was a fisherman.

As Paul Harvey the radio announcer would say, "And here's the rest of the story." After the fishing was done and we were back on shore, the father must have thanked me ten times for the unbelievable trip. I thought he was thanking me for the catch his son made. He explained, though, that his marriage was rocky and his son spent most of his time with his mother. The six hours they'd just been fishing was the most time he had spent with his son in two years.

Joe and his son Bobby came back fishing every year for many years to come. I don't remember any of the other trips, but I do know that Joe's still married to Bobby's mother and Bobby now brings his kids fishing. Can fishing really alter someone's life? I think so!

## IS IT REALLY ABOUT CATCHING?

Mary calls. "My dad would like to go fishing on the Great Lakes but he's in a wheelchair. Can you take us out?"

Since I took Uncle Lloyd out many years back, I figure this can't be much different. We got Dan on the boat by carrying him from the wheelchair. Dan and his two children caught some fish. Dan reeled in two. I knew he was sick with cancer, but at the time I did not know how sick he was. A couple of weeks later I received a letter in the mail from Mary:

Dear Captain Dale:

Just thought you would like to know our father, Dan, passed away five days ago. After our fishing trip it was like he had finished God's work and was ready to move on. He went to the hospital two days after the trip and never came home. Dad made me promise that I would share with you some of his last words before passing on: Mary, thank you so much for taking me fishing with Captain Dale. That had to be one of the most exciting things I've ever done.

How can fishing give people peace of mind? Line in the water. The stories are endless (another book) and the ones I remember are not the biggest, smallest, or the most.

## You never know

It was a calm sunny day, and we left port at 5:30 a.m. The crew: mother, daughter, son-in-law. I did not ask a lot of questions about experience beforehand. We set out all eleven lines and no more than twenty minutes went by when my first mate hollers, "Fish on!"

The son-in-law grabs the pole. It was a fifteen-pound salmon. He's reeling the pole upside down and almost drops the pole in the water. The mother grabs the pole from him and proceeds to reel in the fish. Twenty minutes later the salmon lies flopping on the deck and everyone was high fiving each other. We ended up with eleven fish that day, and the son-in-law never reeled in one of them. He had never fished before; the mother and daughter were the fishermen. Boy, did I learn that day not to prejudge anyone on board.

## RENEWED MEANING IN LIFE

"Captain Dale, would you be willing to take out some physically challenged people on your boat for free? We have an outing once a year and take out twenty to twenty-five physically challenged people out for a day." The answer was a quick yes.

Turned out they needed six boats to accommodate everyone. Our boat had two people with canes and two in wheelchairs. After we'd loaded everyone on board, someone handed me a camera and told me to take pictures of fish.

The seas were as calm as I had ever seen them. The good Lord must have known about the people on board. Soon the call came: "Fish on!" The four people had drawn cards to see who went first. Mike, who was in a wheelchair, was up. We handed him the pole and locked the wheels on his chair. He managed to reel for over 15 minutes until he landed a twelve-pound salmon. I have fished my whole life, but have never even seen so much excitement among a group of people. I took pictures of everyone and forgot to take pictures of fish! Everyone agreed that if no one else caught a fish, it was the best fishing day of their lives. Just to see Mike land that fish made it all worthwhile.

As the day ended, each person had caught two fish and missed many others. I had taken all twenty-four pictures on the throwaway camera. The good Lord was with us all that day. We arrived back at port and the four fishermen bragged about how they had reeled in their fish all by themselves. Afterward all the captains and fishermen met for a lunch. I handed my camera to the leader and said, "Lots of pictures, but none of fish." One of the other boats came in with zero fish. (It just wasn't their day). He gave his camera back to the leader and said, "I didn't take any pictures. We didn't get any fish." How sad that he just didn't get it.

## GRANDKIDS SHOW GRANDPA

"Captain Dale, I know it's only June but I would like to book a trip with my grandsons for August."

August came soon enough. We left port, a proud grandpa and two grandkids whose ages were about twelve and fourteen. It was a cloudy day with one to two foot waves. Very fishable, but a storm had gone through the night before. I warned that catching might be slow due to the weather pattern. The boys flipped a coin to see who would reel in the first fish. Joey the youngest caught the biggest. Two hours of fishing, three bites but no takers, and then, "Fish on!"

This was not just a fish but a monster fish. Joey grabbed the pole. He reeled for thirty minutes and then gave the pole to Mike. He reeled for twenty minutes, and finally it lay on the deck, a twenty-seven-pound salmon. Biggest fish of the year! You would have thought that Eric and Billy had each won a new bike, they were so excited. And Grandpa looked prouder than a man whose son had just won a gold medal at the Olympics. I took the boys' pictures with the fish and Grandpa, and they e-mailed the pictures immediately to their parents. They have returned many times since, but every time the conversation comes back to, "Remember when we both had to reel in that monster?"

## A FAMILY AFFAIR

My daughter calls and says, "Dad, I have a friend at school, a mother of five children. Can you give them a deal and take them fishing?"

The date was set. The group consisted of dad, mom, and five kids, the oldest fourteen and the youngest seven. The day started as any other trip. We left port at 1:30 p.m. Mom and Dad agreed not to reel in any fish. The youngest asked a million questions about everything and anything. One hour goes by, no fish, and the kids are getting bored.

"Fish on!" the first mate shouts.

There's a fish on another pole–two at once. Each kid reels in a nice rainbow trout. What excitement. The parents seemed more excited than the kids. We put the fish in the cooler. One of the kids who caught the fish asked me whose fish was bigger, his or his brother's? I told him his was. He proceeded to brag to his brother that his fish was bigger, and his brother starts crying. We weighed both fish and they were identical in weight. At least that was what I told them. All five kids and the parents each reeled in a fish that day. Like most kids, by the time we returned to port, all the questions were more about the boat: what type it was, the size, how big the engine was. More questions about the boat than about the fish they had caught, so I wondered ...

Six months later I happened to be at the school for a talk I give to local schools about fishing on the Great Lakes. Three of those five kids were at that school. Afterward all three kids came up to me and described in detail what kind of fish they'd caught. The talked about the size and how long it had taken to reel them in, and of course each one said they had caught the biggest!

## THE BIGGEST FISH EVER

It was late August. We had been fishing close to shore—two hundred yards versus eight or nine miles out, since the fish were staging for the fall run. We had been catching large fish, twenty pounds or so, pretty consistently for five days. Two charters to the day I told my first mate, Smiley, and advised him to get lots of rest that night.

Our first trip in the morning included four people, it was foggy, and the seas were calm. The first salmon was twenty-four pounds. After some shouting and sore hands, a twenty-five pounds salmon lay on deck. Three hours later we had seven fish in the cooler with the smallest one twenty-two pounds. Someone asked when were we going to catch a big one? (The average size is twelve to seventeen pounds.) All of a sudden—"Fish on!" Smiley says to me, "Dale, this is a monster!" Fifty minutes later we've got a thirty-one-pound salmon. Wow! Biggest fish we had ever caught on our boat!

The afternoon charter that day also had four people, and we left port at 1:30. "Captain Dale, what's the biggest fish you landed in your boat this year?" one man, Jim, asked, I proudly responded, "A thirty-one-pound salmon that we caught this morning."

"Well," Gordy said, "we are going to beat that."

Two and a half hours later we'd had no bites, no fish, and then "Fish on! Fish on! Fish on!" Three on at once!

After an hour and a half, three guys were hugging, sharing high fives, and shouting as on the deck lay three salmons. Even Smiley, my first mate, was excited, and if you knew Smiley, you'd know that didn't happen often. We weighed the biggest of the three—thirty-seven pounds! Largest ever landed on my boat. I don't know how Gordy knew it, but he did get the biggest fish that day. Actually, it was the biggest fish of the year.

## CUSTOMER BECOMES FRIEND

"Captain Dale, we're coming to golf for four days at a resort on Lake Michigan. We would like to book a morning charter just two of us."

We had been catching nice rainbows twelve miles to the south for about a week. We left port at 1:30 and were finally set up by 2:30. I said to Jeff and Mike, "When we get close to this area where we have been catching the rainbows, we'll catch fish."

"Captain Dale," Jeff said, "I have been on about twenty charter boats and have heard that line way too many times."

He no more then said that when, yep, "Fish on!" And then, "Fish on!" Jeff said to Smiley, "I heard you the first time," and Smiley said, "No, we have two on at once. Fish on!" Make that three on at once. Every time we went over that spot, we had a fish on. Two and a half hours later we had ten fish in the box, the limit of five each. We headed back to the marina. After Jeff was off the boat, he said, "See you in the morning. By the way, that was the best day fishing I've ever had, so we are not expecting much tomorrow."

I thought the same.

Five thirty the next morning, Jeff and Mike showed up, ready to go. We went to the same spot and four hours later we were back with ten rainbows, all over twelve pounds. I never thought I'd hear a customer say, "I can't reel anymore. My arm is sore!"

## OH SO DIFFERENT PERSONALITIES

I finally have a day off from chartering, so we decide to take out two of our grandsons, Cody and Brady, both fourteen. Cody was a big strapping boy, five ten and two hundred pounds and a size 12 shoe size. Brady was also five ten, but only one hundred and forty pounds and a size 9 shoe size. Cody was passive and Brady very aggressive. Brady was born without a left forearm but he had adapted very well.

After we got out on the lake, the boys tossed a coin to see who would reel in the first fish. Cody won. When we hook the first fish, Cody grabbed the pole. This was a big fish. He reeled for fifteen minutes, and finally Brady allowed Cody to use his shoulder to rest the pole on, since Cody was complaining that it was getting hard to reel. After twenty minutes Brady said to

Cody, "Come on, get that fish in!" Cody said, "Brady, wait till it's your turn. You don't know how hard this is."

Finally we boat the fish, a twenty-two-pound salmon. The boys cheered, and that fast we had another fish. Brady grabbed the pole and propped it in his left elbow and starts reeling. (His left arm extends down to the elbow and about three inches beyond.) Cody asked if he needed help; Brady said no. After twenty minutes we boat the fish.

"Fish on!"

"Cody it's your turn."

"My arms are too sore, Brady. You'll have to reel it in."

So Brady did reel it in, and did so six more times with one hand. Cody never looked at Brady as handicapped, just a little more challenged.

Brady is now first mate on my boat.

## TIME SPENT WITH MY BOY

It was springtime, April to be exact, and my son Bunky and I were fishing for browns right after the ice was out. We used our small sixteen foot boat and light tackle, fishing the shoreline of Lake Michigan. Bunky was twelve years old and had the patience of his father when it came to fishing. At 7 a.m. we were trolling with four lines in the water. By 11:08, no bites, not a one. We decided we'd fish till Noon. If no fish by then, we'd quit.

At 11:15 we had fish on three poles at the same time, all brown trout. By noon we had boated nine fish, all about the same size, eight to ten pounds. Wow, some action. One trout had a nine inch fish in its mouth when we caught it. I said to Bunky, "Let's stay till we get our tenth fish." He agreed. We stayed till 3:00 and went home with … nine fish.

Captain Dale A. Laurin Sr.

## TIME SPENT WITH MY DAUGHTER

"Hey, Dad," my daughter Kelly said, "I'm off work for two days. Take me fishing on Lake Michigan."

"You are in luck," I said. "No charters for three days. Let's stay on the boat and fish."

We drove up to the boat in the late afternoon, talking about life in general. I didn't think we accomplished anything or solved the problems of the world, as they say, but it sure was enjoyable.

We set off at 5:30 the next morning and trolled for four hours. Zero bites. Finally, we got a fish.

"Grab the pole, Kel!"

After thirty-five minutes I slip the net under the fish. It was a seventeen-pound rainbow trout, the biggest of the season.

"Dad, is this a nice one?"

"Kel, you could say that. It is the biggest rainbow of the year. Best take a picture."

We caught two smaller fish that day. We had a great time, just her and I and an awfully nice rainbow!

## BONDING, MANY YEARS LATER

"It was 1985. I had been given a gift certificate for a fishing charter trip for two on Lake Michigan. Even though I lived only forty-five minutes from the lake, I had never been fishing on it. I'm a physician and never took the time to do a lot of outdoor things. But my receptionist booked a day for the trip and also asked my son, also a physician, to go along. We left late afternoon the day before the trip and stayed at a motel. That evening we went for dinner. We both realized that evening that over the last ten years, we had not taken much time to be together and just talk. We talked till early morning hours about family, kids, etc., but not work. I recall we didn't get much sleep that night. You know, I think we caught some fish that day, but I can't tell you how many or how big. I just remember spending time with my son."

## OLD EQUIPMENT

I had bragged the day to my first mate before that I had rods and reels on board that I'd been using for twenty years, and they worked just fine.

This trip was a four-person charter, two couples. We had caught eleven salmon in two hours and everyone was having a good time. It was Mary's turn to reel in a fish again, but after reeling for fifteen minutes she said, "Captain Dale, I can't reel anymore."

"Keep going," I told her. "You can do it."

No, she said. The reel was coming off the pole.

I looked down and the saw the reel was about to come apart from the pole. We quickly fixed the problem. She proceeded to continue fighting the fish, but ten minutes later the reel was lying on the deck and the fish was still on the line. We grabbed the line and proceeded to pull the twenty-three pound fish in hand over hand

It was time to get some new fishing equipment!

# Are there Sailfish in Lake Michigan?

Tim, my brother-in-law, had fished many times on my boat. This time we were looking for rainbow trout. It was a late July day. Conditions were perfect, seas calm, water temp sixty degrees. The best part of catching rainbows is that they normally jump seven times before you finally get them into the boat. We had five in the box and they all jumped five to seven times. Number six jumped three times and was coming way too fast. I told Tim that when it got to the back of the boat, it might surprise us. I was right. When it got to the back of the boat, the fish jumped—no, actually it leaped eight feet into the air and crossed three other lines. What a mess, but somehow we did manage to net the fish. One hour later, after cutting most of the tangled lines, we were back looking for more rainbows. I looked at Tim and said," That last one must have been half sailfish!"

## LIKE OLD TIMES

The call came from one of my long-standing customers and friends, Walt.

"Captain Dale, I want to book a date to fish, he said, but with a twist!! I would like to request that you do not have a first mate on my fishing charter tri. I agreed. Walt was taking his eighty-year-old old father and his brother on a fishing charter.

Walt explained how when he was a kid, his dad would take himself and his brother out on the big pond (Lake Michigan). He wanted it to be just like old times, Dad taking care of the lines and the boys reeling in the fish.

So it went. I let Dad set the lines, change lures, and do all the things the first mate does. He did so without missing a beat, all with a smile as big as a setting sun. Dad told stories of catching big kings from their little boat, and how the engine would give them trouble, about the smell of cigars he had smoked while fishing in the old days, and many other stories the boys had heard hundreds of times. I do not remember how many fish we caught that day, but I do know Dad and the boys had a memory not soon to forget.

Did I mention that it was Walt's dad's eightieth birthday that day? What a birthday present!

## MOM ALWAYS SAID,
## "THINGS COULD ALWAYS BE WORSE"

There is a wonderful organization called Outdoor Challenge. They organize outings for physically challenged people. I volunteered my boat for a fishing outing, along with seven other boats in the marina. As my boat is handicapped accessible, I was assigned a group of three that consisted of one man in a wheelchair who had multiple sclerosis; another man with a walker who had to sit 98 percent of the time, and a Vietnam vet with one prosthetic arm.

It took some time to get them all on board. Five of us had to lift Charlie, the wheelchair guy, onto the boat. Everyone caught fish that day. And each and every one of them reeled in their fish without any assistance, all with the same words: "I can do it."

I never once heard how bad things were or that there were things they could not do. As a matter of fact, Charlie had deer hunted in Montana, deer hunted in Wisconsin, and drove his own van.

We have been now providing my boat for five years in a row for this annual fishing trip, and I continue to do this for a selfish reason. Each year it seems to put my life back into perspective.

After that first trip it has become difficult for me to complain about the fish not biting or the weather turning bad, any of those things that we all know are not all that important in the big scheme of things.

# IS THERE ENOUGH LINE ON THE REEL?

An employer had paid for the trip and four of the company's salesmen were on board our boat. The day was picture perfect, very little wind and the sun was shining. The waters were calm.

We left port with great expectations, and the fishing gods did not let us down. We were able to land four nice king salmon, small for that time of the year, ten to twelve pounds. When it was Mike's turn, he grabbed the pole when the fish bit.

"Just hold on to the pole. Do not reel," my first mate advised.

The fish went and took line and more line. Mike looked at the line counter on the reel, hollering 675 feet, and then 800 feet, 850 feet. "Captain Dale, how much line is on the reel?"

I tell him not to worry. There's plenty of line. Besides, the fish will give up soon. But then the fish reaches nine hundred feet and I can see the end of the line on the reel. Mike shouts—and then the line goes limp.

"Reel as fast as you can," my first mate said.

Mike followed instructions well. He reeled fast then a steady reel for forty-five minutes and finally my first mate puts the fish into the net. Twenty-three pounds! It was the biggest fish of the day—and the last one Mike reeled in. He passed on his turn three times, saying his arm would never be the same.

# NICE GUYS SOMETIMES FINISH LAST

We were fishing in the brown trout derby with some friends and relatives that July day. We headed north seven miles, where we had some luck the day before. The four guys on board drew numbers. Gil went first. He landed a nice ten-pound brown. Randy caught a six pound and Jim got a nice twelve pound. The action was good. No misses so far.

When it was Randy's turn again, he grabbed the pole and just like that, the fish was gone. Not long after that the same pole went off again. Randy grabbed the pole but the same result— no fish. Randy said, "I give up," and headed to the bunk to read a magazine. Half an later the pole went off again. Randy forfeited his turn, telling someone else to take it. Gil grabbed the pole and the fight was on. After all was said and done, Gil landed the fish Randy should have caught. It was a twenty-three pound brown which won him fourth place in the derby and a $500 prize.

"Randy, how was the fishing magazine?" I asked.

"Oh, just shut up."

## YES, I HAVE LICENSE, SIR

We were fishing for perch, our seventeen-month old daughter, my pregnant wife, and me. Sis sat in a lawn chair, straddling the seat. We were catching some perch, as many as we could with a toddler in the boat and my bride not to mobile.

A boat came very close to us—a game warden. He asked to see our fishing licenses. I fumbled for my wallet and handed it over to him. He turned to Sis and asked for hers. She tried to reach down for her purse but in her condition, she couldn't reach it. She asked me to come to the front of the boat to help her while the warden repeated, "Ma'am, I need to see your license!" She explained that she was nine months pregnant and was trying to reach my purse but couldn't. At that point, our seventeen-month-old devil in disguise started crying and screaming. I guess with all that commotion the warden had had enough.

"Ma'am, do you have a fishing license?"

"Yes, I do."

"Good enough. You guys have a nice day."

## PLANNER BOARDS TO CATCH WALLEYES

It was the early '80s, and my fishing buddy Dan and I were involved in the local walleye tournaments. We never seemed to be in the money, but always a couple of places out of the running.

From the early '70s through the '80s we did a lot of fishing for brown trout on the bay of Green Bay. The technique we used was Rapala fishing lures and eight-pound test line attached to a planner board. We were very successful with this technique. We could run six lines at one time, cover a lot more area, and have fewer tangles.

One year I asked Dan, "Why can't we use planner boards on Lake Winnebago? For walleyes?" he asked. "Let's do it."

So we did. Everyone that knew us said we were crazy. They said you had to fish on the reefs to catch walleye. You cannot catch walleye in the middle of the lake.

Well, we were right. We did catch fish in the middle of the lake and we did finally win some money in the tournament. That was the start of the world of planner boards for walleye.

Unfortunately for Dan and me, we were not smart enough to market our idea of planner boards. Someone else grabbed the idea and got a sponsor and became the guy that revolutionized the fishing industry. Whenever I hear stories of planner boards used for walleye fishing, I grin a little and move on.

# HOW SPOILED SOME OF US CAN GET

Mike had been fishing on the big pond with me for some years now. He had two daughters, and after many trips he asked me if he could bring his girls out the next time? I agreed, even though I thought they seemed a little young at six and eight. Well, I'm sure glad they came out. They were the good-luck girls. It seemed like every time they came out, they caught ten to eighteen big salmon. Most of the time, the girls would reel in the fish by themselves with a little help from Dad. All in all, they were very good fishermen.

So it went at least two times a year for many years. Each and every trip it was the same—lots of fish.

Apparently they thought everyone that fished Lake Michigan caught fifteen fish each time. One trip, not too long ago Mike and his daughters came out on one of their trips. When the day was over we had caught what for me was an average day, nine fish. On our way in, the girls said to Mike, "Boy, we sure didn't have a very good day catching fish today, did we, Dad?" Mike explained how lucky they had been all those years, and that there were days he fished on the lake and didn't catch anything. I think to this day they still don't really believe that someone could go fishing for salmon on Lake Michigan and not catch a single salmon. If they only knew!

# AGAIN, IT IS NOT ABOUT THE CATCHING

Jeff had been out with a couple of friends the previous year. They had days of exceptional rainbow trout catching. Two trips limit each day!

He mentioned when he was leaving that next year, he's booking three trips in one week.

Jeff did follow up with his promise of three charters the next year. Unfortunately, our first two trips were not even close to the limits they had caught the last year.

For the last trip Jeff brought this young guy with him and introduced him as his son Eric from Madison, Wisconsin. As the day unfolded I found that Jeff and Eric did not see a lot of each other, but they seemed to enjoy each other's company. Fishing was slow. Jeff and Eric had each reeled in one fish. It was Eric's first Great-Lake salmon and he was proud of the accomplishment. The seas were calm, the sun was shining, and it was getting hot. Most boats had moved on to other areas to fish; we were the only boat left.

Then, fish on! My first mate, Brady, grabbed the pole and handed it to Eric. After a twenty-minute fight, the twenty-three-pound salmon was in the net. Eric was so excited he could not catch his breath. Jeff took many pictures of his son holding his trophy.

The day ended and we headed back to port. I overheard Eric say, "Dad thanks you so much for taking me out on this trip. It really means a lot to me. I think we should make this an annual event."

Jeff responded, "That would be nice."

I'm not sure, but I think I saw a tear in both Jeff's and Eric's eyes. No more was said, but I sure could feel the bonding going on.

## SHE LEARNED WELL

My older daughter Kelly had been on so many fish trips on Lake Michigan, I lost track. Her mother and I not only taught her how to fish but also to clean fish. Actually, she and her brother were in charge of cleaning our catch. The one they disliked most was cleaning smelt. To clean smelt, you use scissors and a toothbrush. You cut the heads off with the scissors and then clean out the insides with the toothbrush. (Always throw away the toothbrush when done!)

Kelly married a man fifteen years older than herself. She believed he was quite the outdoors man; she found out later that this was not the case.

They did go out fishing a few times but with little success. On one occasion they did catch a northern and some perch. When they got home Kel asked her husband if he wanted her to clean the fish. I guess in his family there was no such thing as a woman cleaning fish, so he said to her, "Sure, try it." As she was filleting the northern, she asked him if he wanted her to take out the bones. He said, "No one knows how to do that, but try it." So she did, and when all the fish were done there were no bones or skin. (She had skinned them also.) He was dumbfounded.

"Where in God's name did you learn to clean fish like that?"

She just said, "Lots of experience …"

## FREE FISH

My younger daughter, Kerry Jo, was never interested in fishing when she was young, or even as she developed into a wonderful adult. Fact of the matter is, she did not even like to eat fish. We took her fishing like the other two but it was punishment to her, not enjoyment.

Kerry got married and had three wonderful children. As her oldest, Cody, started fishing with me at a young age, I encouraged her to keep the salmon we caught. Finally she tried cooking it on the grill. "Dad, the fish is excellent. I'll take all you can get."

So many years we had perch dinners and she would eat peanut butter sandwiches, or peanut butter and crackers instead of fish.

Just little background on the cost of fishing equipment for our fishing boat. One rod and reel setup: $200 -$300. Each lure: $6-7 apiece. The cost of fuel per trip: $130. Electronics: $5,000 and boat: $85,000. Insurance $3000., dockage fees $1200., incidentals $1000.

One day Kerry Jo my youngest daughter calls me up and says, "Dad, I was in the grocery store today and they were selling fresh Atlantic salmon for $14 a pound! Can you believe that, Dad? That's unbelievable when **you** get it for **free**!"

I just smiled.

# BIG MISTAKE

It was a calm day on the water. My wife, daughter, and son—who were twelve and ten—were fishing for walleye on our favorite lake, Bago. The fish were biting and we had our limit for the day. And like most days, the fish seemed to be in one spot. This was long before electronics, so we had to mark spots on the water the old-fashioned way: a plastic milk jug with a string tied to it and a weight on the end of the string. Once we located the active fish, we would throw out the jug and then either troll or drift over the area.

We had our limit of fish and it was time to leave. I started the motor and headed for our milk-jug marker. My son's job was to reach over from the bow of the boat and grab the marker. He had done this a hundred times. As

I'm getting closer, I can see it unfold before my eyes. Before I can say a word my son reaches for the marker but cannot reach it and falls out of the boat. Fortunately he was wearing his life jacket. His mother panics and moves to the same side of the boat. I turn off the motor and lean to the opposite side of the boat. I tell everyone to be calm. I instruct my son to hang onto the side of the boat and work his way to the back of the boat. Once he's at the stern, I instruct him to climb up the back of the boat using the bottom of the motor as a ladder. He does this and it all works out. He is back in the boat, but I can see he is shaken up. We head for home. Later that day we discuss the episode and I give everyone instructions on what not to do.

The next day I get up to go fishing. I wake up my son and he tells me he doesn't want to go fishing. *What's that?* I say to myself. Well, so be it. There were three more invitations over three days and three more no's from my son.

Now it's time to get him back into the boat. The next Saturday I wake him again to go fishing; again he says no. I force him to go. Once at the boat landing he refuses to get into the boat. I literally carry him onto the boat. By the time we get to the fishing grounds, his fear is gone. While fishing that day he tells me he was glad he came. (A son's way of saying thanks.)

At the end of the day he was again in charge of picking up the jug. This time as we got closer he hollered to me that he couldn't reach it and I should turn around and let him try again. I think this was the one and only time I did not lecture him on the word *can't*. Somehow it seemed like the proper time to use that word.

# FINAL NOTE

My wish is that after you have read this book, you can relate at least to one small area covered in it. But more importantly, I hope you learned what it took me so many years to learn. No matter what you are doing in life, whether it's work or play, attending a function you really don't want to be at or doing something you love—like fishing maybe—tell yourself over and over again: **<u>Enjoy The Moment!</u>**

I leave you all with this final note: I wish I could say this was my idea but I recently read this in a Wisconsin Natural Resource magazine: "I do believe that if more people spent more time fishing, the world would be a different place. You see when some people go to the temple of God to pray, they sit and think of fishing instead of thinking of God. I like to go fishing and think of all the wonderful things God has created for us to enjoy and be thankful for all that he has done."

Grandson Cody all grown up.

Grandson Kenny and big smallmouth bass
while on our annual trip to Canada.

Dan on left and crazy Cousin Ernie on right.
Dan, Ernie, and I introduced the planner-
board approach to fishing for walleyes.

Bunky, my son, on a guided trip back when he
was twelve years old. He was in charge of driving
the boat. "Bunky, where the hell are you going?"

Some browns from the first of our many
trips on the bay with Cousin Ernie.

My older sister Lois. Yes, she really did turn
into a fisherman. She is holding a state-record
Splake ( a cross between a lake trout and a
brook trout). Her brother never registered
the fish for her. What are brothers for?

Bunky apparently not so happy with his catch.
Or was his dad hollering at him all day again?

I could not leave this one out of my book. This is my cousin Jim, Ernie's older brother. After he retired from teaching he drove my boat for me in the summer. He had to be one of the funniest men ever put on this earth, no matter what subject he talked about he would make you laugh. At the age of sixty-five he went to the big pond in the sky. Jim, this one is for you. We miss you so. The picture says it all!

Picture presented to me by one of the girls
who always had great luck on board. She took
first place at school with this picture of sunrise
on Lake Michigan. Congrats, Hannah.

Another of Hannah's pictures.

My grandson Cody on the left and little
Kelly on the right. Kelly was one of
many first mates throughout the years.
He was one of the really good ones.

Oldest daughter Kelly Ann with her monster
fifteen-pound rainbow. She's now teaching
her son how to fish. LIW. It does work.

Some of the grandkids. left to right: Kenny,
Katie, Rachel, and Brady, the same Brady
that is now my first mate. The girls will
never forget this trip. Not because of all the
fish, but they were seasick the whole time.

This is my best friend, Burdock. He is always
grouchy around me. But we always have fun
when we're together. We have been friends
now for over fifty years. Boy, are we lucky.

This is a classic. These are some northern pike that were caught on that little lake that engulfed me for several minutes and allowed me to meet my guardian angel. The fish were caught around 1962. Burdock and I got these on a hot summer day.

Brady, my current first mate, with a nice catch, fishing on a day off.

Brady on left and Cody on right. My
grandsons on another fishing trip.

Brady and Cody. Who is helping whom?

Present-day charter boat.

Grandson Ian proud of big fish #1.

Granddaughter Katie. Nice one. Yeah!

Granddaughter Kylie Jo. A fun day as usual.

Grandson Robbie. One of many
fish caught that day.

Youngest daughter Kerry Jo, her
3 children and my bride.

# ABOUT THE AUTHOR

This is Dale's second published book. The first one was A5- Second high... The Wisconsin Tradition: "The Deer Hunt"

Dale was born in the Upper Peninsula of Michigan and had moved with his family, to Wisconsin at an early age. Since that time he has been a lifetime resident of Wisconsin residing in Fox Valley, which consist of the cities of Neenah, Menasha, and Appleton. He has been married for forty-five years and has three children and ten grandchildren.

When not fishing or writing, Dale volunteers at many of the local schools demonstrating such things as: Fishing secrets, How to make maple syrup, and How to build snowshoes for under $10. He loves freshwater fishing, ice fishing, snowshoeing, deer hunting, small game hunting, downhill skiing, cross country skiing, hiking and kayaking. In his" spare" time he builds Cedar strip kayaks, Stand-up paddleboards, as well as Rustic pine log furniture, built from trees he planted twenty years ago. Dale also does wood relief carving, as well as Leather art burning. Dale also has a small maple syrup farm in northern Wisconsin.

He and his bride of 45 yrs are "Cruisers". They have been to such places as the Panama Canal, Nova Scotia, and 10 trips to Alaska. They also have travelled throughout all 50 of the United States.

# ABOUT THE BOOK

There are secrets to catching fish, but there are also secrets to everyday living. This book covers a vast number of both subjects.

It tells of a young boy who discovered his passion at an early age—fishing—and the secrets he learned along the way. But what he did not know was that those secrets he learned at an early age about fishing actually applied to everyday life. Things like raising children or becoming a successful salesman or handling stress. Over the years he found that fishing secrets had many applications to life in general.

The book is not just about fishing but how our lives are interwoven with all the activities we are involved in throughout our lives.